Pavin

GCSE

Geography Revision Guide

Improving understanding through colour and clarity

Get your FREE digital book!

This book includes a free digital edition for use on computers (PC and Mac), tablets or smartphones.

Go to ddedu.co.uk/geography and enter this code...

Code: DPPYQX83

GCSE Geography

Contents

Natural Hazards

Natural hazards are naturally occurring events that pose a risk to human life and property. The type, frequency and magnitude of the hazard affect the severity of the risk.

Types of Natural Hazard

Natural hazards are often classified by their cause:

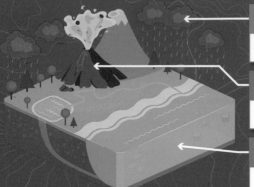

Atmospheric – caused by atmospheric conditions (weather)

Tropical storms	Extreme heat or cold	Climate change

Geophysical – caused by the movement of tectonic plates

Volcanoes	Earthquakes	Tsunamis

Hydrological – caused by the occurrence, movement and distribution of water

Flooding	Landslides	Droughts

Many hazards are interrelated; for example, landslides can result from hydrological or geographical causes.

Factors Affecting Hazard Risk

Hazard risk is the likelihood of a natural hazard occurring. There are several factors that can affect hazard risk and make people more vulnerable, including:

Population Density

Areas at risk from natural hazards are becoming more densely populated. The more people living in high-risk areas, the greater the probability of them being affected by natural hazards.

Deforestation

Destroying large areas of forest can increase the risk of natural hazards such as flooding, landslides and drought.

Wealth

Lower-income countries (LICs) often have more people living in high-risk areas. For example, large slums may be built in areas prone to flooding or landslides. LICs may also have less capacity than higher-income countries (HICs) to cope with disasters.

Climate Change

Climate change gives rise to more volatile weather. For example, rising temperatures can increase the risk of tropical storms and drought. Also, wetter seasons can increase the frequency and severity of flooding in some areas.

Disaster Risk Equation

The risk of disaster is higher if:
- the frequency or severity of **hazards** increases
- the **vulnerability** of people increases
- the **capacity to cope** decreases

$$\text{Risk} = \frac{\text{Hazards} \times \text{Vulnerability}}{\text{Capacity to Cope}}$$

daydream
EDUCATION

Global Atmospheric Circulation

Large-scale wind circulations occur over the Earth's surface. These circulations result from differences in air pressure due to the unequal heating of the Earth's surface.

Wind is caused by differences in the atmospheric pressure. When there is a difference, air moves from an area of high pressure to an area of low pressure, resulting in winds. The greater the difference in pressure, the stronger the winds.

Towards the poles, the Sun's energy spreads over a large area, resulting in low temperatures and low pressure.

At the Equator, the Sun's energy is concentrated over a small area, resulting in high temperatures and low pressure.

This difference in air pressure on the Earth's surface causes global patterns of air circulations (**cells**) from areas of high pressure to areas of low pressure.

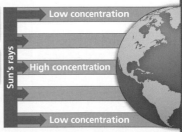

Global Atmospheric Circulation Model

There are three convection cells in each hemisphere: Hadley, Ferrel and Polar cells.

1 Warm air rises from the Equator, creating a belt of low pressure. As the air rises, it cools.

2 The resulting condensation creates clouds and rain that move north and south of the Equator.

3 At 30° north and south of the Equator, the cold, dry air sinks, creating high pressure and clear skies.

4 When the sinking air reaches the Earth's surface, it moves either back to the Equator or towards the poles.

5 At 60° north and south of the Equator, the surface air meets colder air from the poles, which causes it to rise, creating a belt of low pressure.

6 The air rises and cools. At a high level, this moves either back to the Equator or towards the poles.

7 At the poles, the cool air sinks to the Earth's surface, creating high pressure. The air then moves back towards the Equator.

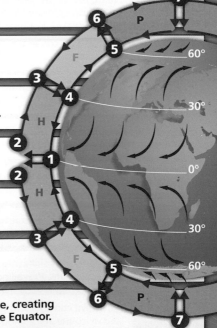

Tropical Storms

Tropical storms are extreme low-pressure weather systems that cause severe winds and torrential rain.

Global Distribution of Tropical Storms

Conditions required:

🌡️ **Ocean Temperature:**
>26°C

🌊 **Water Depth:**
60-70 m

📍 **Location:**
Between 5° and 30° north and south of the Equator

Season:
☀️ Late summer
🍂 Early autumn

Hurricanes · Hurricanes · Typhoons · Equator · Cyclones · Cyclones

🟦 Tropical storms
⬆️ Typical paths

Tropical storms cannot form more than 30° north or south of the Equator as the water is not warm enough and the Coriolis force (spin) not great enough.

Tropical storms have different names depending on their geographical location: they are known as **cyclones** in the Indian and South Pacific Oceans, **hurricanes** in the Atlantic and Eastern Pacific Oceans and **typhoons** in the west of the North Pacific Ocean.

Formation of Tropical Storms

1 Warm, moist, unstable air above the ocean rises, creating an area of low pressure below.

2 Surrounding cooler air is drawn into the area of low pressure, causing winds.

3 The cool drawn-in air now warms up and takes on moisture, causing it to rise.

4 The large mass of rising, warm air cools and condenses, forming large cumulonimbus clouds and heavy rain.

5 Latent heat released during condensation helps to power the storm.

6 As more air is drawn into the area of low pressure, the Earth's rotation causes wind to spiral into the storm's centre, or eye.

7 Colder, drier air sinks into the centre (eye) of the storm, creating calm conditions. Prevailing winds then push the storm towards land.

8 The storm continues to get bigger and stronger until it reaches land or colder seas. Landfall and friction slow the storm down.

Structure and Features of Tropical Storms

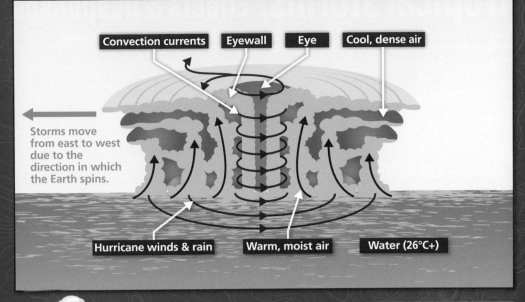

Convection currents | Eyewall | Eye | Cool, dense air

Storms move from east to west due to the direction in which the Earth spins.

Hurricane winds & rain | Warm, moist air | Water (26°C+)

The Coriolis Force

Due to the Earth's curved surface and rotation, the Coriolis force causes winds to bend and cyclones to spin.

In the northern hemisphere, the winds curve to the right, causing storms to swirl in a clockwise direction. In the southern hemisphere, the winds curve to the left, causing storms to swirl in an anticlockwise direction.

Climate Change and Tropical Storms

Climate change is heating the world's oceans and causing sea levels to rise. What effect does this have on the distribution, frequency and intensity of tropical storms?

Frequency
It is thought that the frequency of tropical storms may remain the same or decrease as the Earth gets warmer. However, it is believed that more storms will be classed as severe (category 4 or 5) and last for a longer time.

Intensity
Evidence shows that as sea temperatures rise, storms will become more intense. The increased heat energy powers the storms, bringing higher rainfall and stronger winds. Rising sea levels place coastal areas at greater risk of flooding from tropical storms.

Distribution
As sea temperatures rise, more of the world's oceans will heat to above 27°C. Tropical storms may therefore be able to develop in areas further north or south of the Equator.

Tropical Storms: Effects & Responses

Tropical storms can have a major impact on people and the environment. As with any natural disaster, people must be prepared and ready to respond quickly.

Effects of Tropical Storms

A tropical storm and its associated strong winds and heavy rainfall are likely to have many effects on a location, including flooding, landslides and storm surges.

Primary Effects (Immediate Impacts)

- High rainfall and storm surges lead to flooding, particularly in coastal regions and flood plains.
- Buildings and transport links are destroyed by flooding and high winds.
- People are injured and killed by flooding and debris.
- Water supplies are contaminated by overflowing sewage.
- Electricity cables and communications networks are destroyed by flooding and high winds.
- Food shortages can result from the destruction of crops and livestock.
- People are displaced or made homeless.

Secondary Effects (Long-Term Impacts)

- Disease spreads easily because of contaminated water and poor sanitation.
- Food shortages can result from the destruction of crops and livestock.
- Damage to infrastructure such as roads and power supplies may take a long time to repair.
- The loss of tourism and trade can damage the region's economy.
- Heavy rainfall can trigger landslides, causing further devastation.

The severity of a tropical storm's effects will depend on the storm's size, strength and location. If the location is densely populated, has a poor infrastructure or a poorly prepared population, the effects are likely to be more severe. The area is said to be vulnerable.

daydream EDUCATION

Responses to Tropical Storms

Some effects of tropical storms must be met with an immediate response. Others can be dealt with in the long term.

Immediate Responses

- Evacuate anybody at risk before the storm, potentially to higher ground.
- Rescue any survivors and treat injuries.
- Prevent the spread of disease by recovering any dead bodies.
- Set up temporary shelters for the homeless.
- Provide temporary supplies of food, water and electricity, as well as communications, to those in need.
- Send aid workers, supplies, equipment and financial help to the people affected.

Long-Term Responses

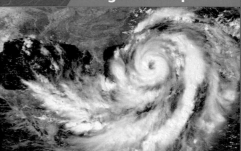

- Rehouse those who have lost their homes.
- Repair or rebuild damaged buildings.
- Improve structural design to help protect buildings against future storms.
- Improve forecasting and warning systems.
- Improve flood defence systems.
- Boost the economy by promoting investment in the area. If the area is suitable, tourism can also create jobs and business opportunities.
- Restore water, energy and gas supplies, and reconnect communication links.

The Three Ps: Prediction, Protection and Planning

Tropical storms can be predicted, so having effective prediction, planning and protection systems can significantly reduce the effects of storms.

Prediction
- Scientists use technology to predict when and where a storm is likely to occur.
- Hurricane warnings give people advice on the necessary actions to take (e.g. evacuation).

Protection
- Buildings can be constructed from reinforced concrete or built on stilts to protect against winds and flooding.
- Flood defences (e.g. levees and sea walls) can be built along rivers and coasts.

Planning
- Disaster kits can be provided for people in high-risk areas.
- Evacuation routes can help to get people away from danger quickly.

Tropical Storms: Typhoon Haiyan

Typhoon Haiyan is one of the most intense tropical cyclones on record. In 2013, it caused widespread devastation to large areas of South East Asia, particularly the Philippines.

Timeline

5th November
Fuelled by high sea surface temperatures, the depression develops into a small typhoon.

7th November
With winds of 190 mph, the typhoon reaches its peak intensity as it hits the Philippines.

3rd November
A low pressure system develops into a tropical depression over the Western Pacific Ocean.

6th November
Rapid intensification continues and a super typhoon forms.

9th - 11th November
The typhoon moves westerly over the South China Sea and dissipates as it hits Vietnam and China.

Typhoon Haiyan

The Philippines

The Philippines is a low-income country (LIC) that is highly susceptible to tropical storms.

With a high population density and many people living in poorly constructed wooden buildings, the Philippines was severely affected by Typhoon Haiyan.

Village on water, Philippines

Typhoon Haiyan destruction

Primary Effects

- Heavy rainfall (400 mm) and a 5-metre storm surge caused severe flooding.
- Infrastructure (e.g. hospitals, airports and roads) was damaged.
- An oil spill caused damage along the coast.
- There were over 6,000 fatalities.
- Homes and buildings were destroyed, with over 2 million people made homeless.
- Widespread power outages occurred.

Secondary Effects

- Large areas of agricultural land were flooded, resulting in crop failure and food shortages.
- Contaminated flood water led to the spread of disease.
- The overall damage was estimated to be £10 billion.

Primary Responses

- Around 800,000 people were evacuated to temporary shelters.
- Over £100 million worth of aid was sent, including food, water and medicine.
- The distribution of aid was slow because of the scale of damage to the country's infrastructure.
- A curfew was introduced to prevent looting.

Secondary Responses

- New legislation was introduced to prevent construction in high-risk areas.
- A new disaster early warning system was developed.
- The government announced a four-year, £6.2 billion plan to rebuild homes, businesses and infrastructure.

daydream EDUCATION

UK Weather Hazards

There are various types of extreme weather that affect the UK.

Drought

A prolonged period of abnormally low rainfall, leading to a shortage of water

Potential Impacts:

- Crop failure can lead to higher food prices, lower incomes for farmers and reliance on food imports.
- Water conservation regulations, such as hosepipe bans, may be introduced, which can affect businesses and householders.

Heavy Rain

A period of abnormally heavy rain

Potential Impacts:

- Short periods of intense rain can cause flash floods. Prolonged rain saturates the ground, which can lead to river flooding.
- Damage may occur to buildings, transport links, communication links and energy supplies.
- Flooded farmland kills crops and animals.
- Repairs often cost millions and can take years to complete.
- Businesses and homeowners in high-risk areas may be denied insurance.

Heatwaves

A prolonged period of abnormally hot weather

Potential Impacts:

- Fatalities and health issues, such as heat exhaustion and breathing difficulties, can occur.
- Road surfaces can melt and rail lines can deform, disrupting transport.
- Crops wither and scorch, which may lead to higher food prices, lower incomes for farmers and reliance on food imports.

Gales

A period of strong, sustained surface winds (common in the west and in upland and coastal regions)

Potential Impacts:

- Buildings, transport links and electricity lines may be damaged.
- Fallen trees and large branches block roads and cause injury.

Extreme Cold Weather

A period of abnormally cold weather leading to snow and ice

Potential Impacts:

- Travel disruptions and safety concerns force businesses and schools to close.
- Food shortages may occur.
- People may become hypothermic and die.
- Slippery conditions cause an increase in fall-related injuries.
- Councils have to spend money on salting, gritting and snow ploughing.
- Crops may be damaged and livestock killed.

Thunderstorms

A heavy rain storm accompanied by thunder and lightning, caused by hot and humid conditions (common in the south-east)

Potential Impacts:

- Lightning can cause fires, electricity surges, fatalities and damage to buildings.
- Flash flooding due to heavy rainfall can damage buildings and transport links.
- Associated winds and hail may damage crops and buildings.

Evidence shows that the weather in the UK is becoming more extreme.

- Temperatures are becoming more extreme: 2014 was the warmest year since 1910, and December 2014 was the coldest month for over 100 years.
- Rainfall is heavier, and storms are more intense and frequent. December 2015 was the wettest UK month on record.

daydream EDUCATION

UK Weather Hazard:
Somerset Levels Flooding, 2013–14

Somerset Levels

Causes

The Somerset Levels is a 650 km² area in the south-west of England. It is made up of mostly low-level farmland, which is vulnerable to tidal and river flooding.

- During autumn and winter 2013–14, powerful Atlantic jet streams drove low-pressure storms from the Atlantic Ocean over the UK, causing prolonged periods of heavy rainfall.

- In December 2013, the monthly rainfall was twice the monthly average, saturating the ground and causing the Parrett and Tone rivers to flood.

- The rivers had not been dredged in over 20 years. Built-up sediment had reduced their capacities and increased flood risk.

- Further storms in February led to more flooding.

Effects

The flooding of the Somerset Levels had social, economic and environmental effects.

Social	Economic	Environmental
• Many villages were inaccessible, except by boat. • Schools were closed. • Flooding caused damage to over 600 homes. • There were power outages in several areas. • Residents were evacuated to temporary housing for several months.	• Businesses were forced to close. • Road and rail links were damaged. • Around 115 km² of farmland remained flooded for over two months, ruining crops. • The total economic cost of the floods was over £145 million.	• Sewage, chemical and oil pollution in floodwater contaminated the land. • Stagnant, deoxygenated water damaged habitats and ecosystems. • Debris from the floodwater littered the region.

Management Strategies

The flood prompted authorities to undertake long-term planning to prevent future events and limit their effects. They worked to create an effective **prediction, planning** and **protection** system.

Somerset County Council spent £20 million on a 20-year flood plan.	Road levels were raised to prevent disruptions to transportation networks.	Rivers were dredged and improvements made to riverbanks and pumps.	Work was carried out to increase the capacity of the King Sedgemoor Drain.

Tectonic Hazards

Tectonic hazards are caused by the movement of tectonic plates in the Earth's crust.

Plate Tectonic Theory

The Earth's surface (crust) is divided into slabs of rock called tectonic plates. These plates are made up of two types of crust; oceanic and continental. Oceanic crust is thin and dense, whereas continental crust is thick and less dense.

Some people believe that convection currents in the mantle cause tectonic plates to move. However, more recent research suggests that movement is caused by **ridge push** and **slab pull**.

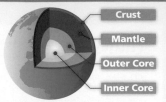

Crust

Mantle

Outer Core

Inner Core

Ridge push occurs at constructive plate margins where newly formed dense oceanic crust slides down away from the plate margin, pushing the plates apart. **Slab pull** occurs at destructive plate margins where denser oceanic crust subducts under continental crust due to gravity, pulling the rest of the plate with it.

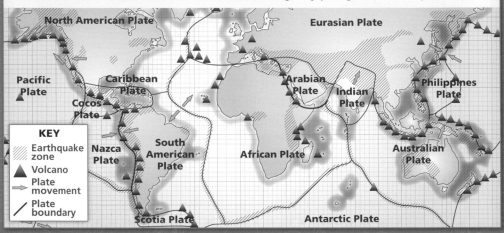

North American Plate

Eurasian Plate

Pacific Plate

Caribbean Plate

Arabian Plate

Indian Plate

Philippines Plate

Cocos Plate

KEY

/// Earthquake zone

▲ Volcano

⇒ Plate movement

/ Plate boundary

Nazca Plate

South American Plate

African Plate

Australian Plate

Scotia Plate

Antarctic Plate

There are three types of plate margin: **constructive**, **destructive** and **conservative**.

Constructive Margins

A constructive plate margin occurs where two plates (oceanic or continental) move apart.

1 Plates move apart.

2 Hot magma rises as plates separate.

4

3

North American Plate ← **1** | **1** → Eurasian Plate

2

Mantle

3 Magma cools and hardens, forming new crust and a ridge.

4 There is relatively gentle volcanic activity.

daydream
EDUCATION

Destructive Margins

A destructive plate margin occurs where an oceanic plate and a continental plate converge (meet).

1 Denser oceanic plate sinks beneath continental plate.

4 Magma rises through continental plate, causing fierce volcanic eruptions.

Fold mountains

Ocean trench

4

South American Plate (continental)

Nazca Plate (oceanic) **1**

2

2 Plates jam, and when pressure is released, violent earthquakes occur.

Mantle

Subduction zone

3

3 Oceanic plate melts.

Where two continental plates converge, neither plate sinks. Instead, the pressure causes the ground to fold and push upwards, forming fold mountains.

Conservative Margins

A conservative margin occurs where plates move past each other in different directions or at different speeds.

San Andreas Fault

Pacific Plate

North American Plate

1 One plate is moving quicker than the other.

Mantle

2 Plates jam, and when pressure is released, violent earthquakes occur.

There are no volcanic eruptions at conservative plate margins.

Mid-Atlantic Ridge
Constructive Margin

The Mid-Atlantic Ridge is a result of the Eurasian and North American plates moving apart. In Iceland, volcanic activity is causing the land area to grow, and the ridge is responsible for hundreds of earthquakes each week.

Ring of Fire
Destructive Margin

The numerous subduction zones around the edge of the Pacific Plate make the Ring of Fire extremely prone to volcanic eruptions and earthquakes.

San Andreas Fault
Conservative Margin

The San Andreas Fault runs along the margin of the North American and Pacific plates. The pressure caused by the plates sliding past each other – in the same direction but at different speeds – results in violent earthquakes.

daydream
EDUCATION

Volcanoes

A volcano is formed when lava, ash and gases break through an opening in the Earth's surface.

Causes of Volcanoes

Volcanoes are found at both destructive and constructive plate margins.

Shield volcanoes are found primarily at **constructive plate margins**. Magma is thin and runny **(non-viscous)**, so eruptions are gentle and the lava can travel long distances. As a result, these volcanoes have shallow sides.

Composite volcanoes are found primarily at **destructive plate margins**. Magma is thick and sticky **(viscous)**, so eruptions are explosive and lava cannot travel far. As a result, these volcanoes have steep sides.

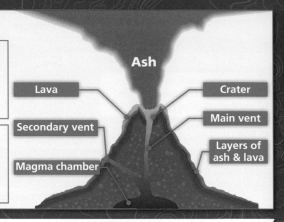

Ash

Lava

Crater

Secondary vent

Main vent

Layers of ash & lava

Magma chamber

Effects of Volcanoes

Volcanic eruptions have both **primary** and **secondary** effects.

Primary Effects (Immediate Impacts)

- Buildings, structures and homes are destroyed by lava and pyroclastic flows.
- Communication and transport links are disrupted.
- People and animals are injured or killed by falling debris, lava, poisonous or suffocating gases, or pyroclastic flows.
- People are left homeless.
- Crops and water supplies are contaminated by falling ash.

Secondary Effects (Long-Term Impacts)

- Pyroclastic flows can burn and destroy forests.
- Emergency aid may not reach those in need for extended periods.
- If volcanic material combines with water, destructive mudslides (lahars) and landslides can occur. Also, flooding can occur as lava melts any ice or snow.
- Disease can spread because of contaminated water and poor sanitation.
- Reconstruction can be costly. Furthermore, lost tourism and trade can damage the local economy.

daydream
EDUCATION

Global Distribution of Volcanoes

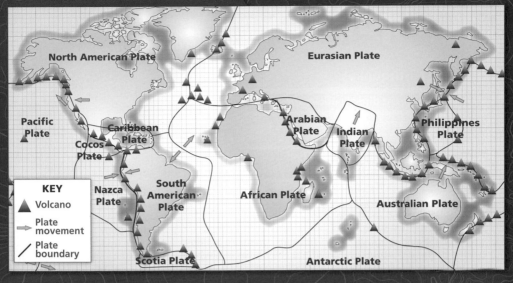

North American Plate

Eurasian Plate

Pacific Plate

Caribbean Plate

Cocos Plate

Arabian Plate

Indian Plate

Philippines Plate

Nazca Plate

South American Plate

African Plate

Australian Plate

Scotia Plate

Antarctic Plate

KEY

▲ Volcano

→ Plate movement

/ Plate boundary

Responses to Volcanoes

Some effects of volcanic eruptions must be met with an immediate response. Others can be dealt with in the long term.

Immediate Responses

- Evacuate anybody at risk, rescue any survivors and treat injuries.
- Extinguish any fires.
- Send aid workers, supplies, equipment and financial help to people affected.
- Recover any dead bodies.
- Set up temporary shelters (e.g. tents) for the homeless.
- Provide temporary supplies of food, water and energy, as well as communications, to those in need.

Long-Term Responses

- Rehouse those who have lost their homes.
- Reconstruct or repair damaged buildings.
- Improve monitoring and evacuation plans for any future disasters.
- Restore water, energy and gas supplies, and reconnect communication links.
- Restore transport links.
- Boost the economy by promoting investment in the area. If the area is suitable, tourism can also create jobs and business opportunities.

Earthquakes

Earthquakes occur when there is a sudden release of pressure in the Earth's crust at plate margins. The energy waves created by the release of pressure cause vibrations and movement in the Earth's surface.

Causes of Earthquakes

Epicentre: The point directly above the focus.

Seismic waves: Energy waves created by the release of pressure at the focus.

Focus: The point where pressure is first released, generating the earthquake.

Earthquakes occur at all types of plate margin.

Constructive Plate	Conservative Plate	Destructive Plate
At constructive plate margins, rising magma causes minor earthquakes as the plates move apart.	At conservative plate margins, pressure builds where the plates jam when grinding past each other.	At destructive plate margins, pressure builds as the oceanic plate sinks and jams beneath the continental plate.

Effects of Earthquakes

Earthquakes have both primary and secondary effects.

Primary Effects (Immediate Impacts)

- Buildings, structures and homes are destroyed.
- People and animals are injured or killed by falling buildings or debris.
- Transport and communication links are damaged.
- Supplies of water, electricity and gas are cut off as pipes and cables are destroyed.
- People are left homeless.

Secondary Effects (Long-Term Impacts)

- Gas leaks can cause fires.
- Disease can spread due to poor sanitation.
- Landslides, tsunamis and aftershocks can cause further damage, injury and death.
- Emergency aid may not reach those in need for extended periods.
- Reconstruction can be costly. Moreover, lost tourism and trade can hurt the local economy.

daydream
EDUCATION

Global Distribution of Earthquakes

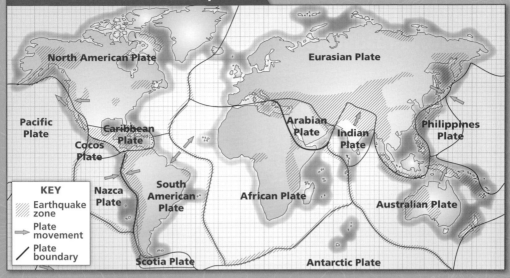

North American Plate

Eurasian Plate

Pacific Plate

Caribbean Plate

Cocos Plate

Arabian Plate

Indian Plate

Philippines Plate

Nazca Plate

South American Plate

African Plate

Australian Plate

Scotia Plate

Antarctic Plate

KEY
- ▨ Earthquake zone
- → Plate movement
- ╱ Plate boundary

Responses to Earthquakes

Some effects of earthquakes must be met with an immediate response. Others can be dealt with in the long term.

Immediate Responses

- Conduct a search and rescue to find people who may be trapped.
- Extinguish any fires.
- Recover any dead bodies.
- Send aid workers, supplies, equipment and financial help to people affected.
- Set up temporary shelters (e.g. tents) for the homeless.
- Provide temporary supplies of food, water and electricity, as well as communications, to those in need.

Long-Term Responses

- Rehouse those who have lost their homes.
- Reconstruct or repair damaged buildings.
- Restore water, energy and gas supplies, and reconnect communication links.
- Improve building regulations and implement plans for more earthquake-resistant buildings.
- Review the effectiveness of responses and update action plans for future events.
- Boost the economy by promoting investment and tourism in the area to create jobs and business opportunities.

Tectonic Hazards:
Areas of Contrasting Wealth

High-income countries (HICs) are often far better equipped to cope with tectonic hazards than low-income countries (LICs) and newly-emerging economies (NEEs).

NEE

Location: 📍
Central Java, Indonesia
When: 📅
25th–26th October 2010
Volcano type: 🗻
Active composite volcano

BORNEO

Java Sea

JAVA ▲ Mount Merapi

ICELAND

● Reykjavik

▲ Eyjafjallajökull

HIC

📍 **Location:**
Eyjafjallajökull, southern Iceland
📅 **When:**
March–May 2010
🗻 **Volcano type:**
Long fissure volcano

Primary Effects

- Pyroclastic flows and hot gases (up to 800°C) reached areas over 11 km away from the volcano.
- Over 350 people were killed.
- Lava flows and ash forced roads to close.
- Around 20,000 people were made homeless.
- Crops and livestock were killed by pyroclastic flows and contamination from volcanic ash.

Mount Merapi

- Volcanic ash contaminated local streams and water supplies, killing plants and animals.
- Over 3,000 tonnes of CO_2 per day were released into the atmosphere.
- Poor visibility and ash forced roads to close.
- Schools and businesses were closed.
- People had to wear face masks and goggles.

Secondary Effects

- Damage to crops drove up food prices.
- The loss of crops and livestock meant farmers lost valuable sources of income.
- The danger area was extended to 20 km.
- Ash, rock and lava were washed into towns by rainfall, causing lahars (volcanic mudflows).
- Overcrowded evacuation centres allowed disease to spread easily.

Aftermath of 2010

- *Jökulhlaups* (glacial floods) were caused by glacial melting.
- The loss of crops and livestock meant farmers lost valuable sources of income.
- Winds carried the ash over Europe, grounding over 100,000 flights. This cost airlines around £130 million per day for eight days.
- Tourism numbers decreased temporarily.

Eyjafjallajökull

Short-Term Responses

- Over 200 temporary evacuation centres (e.g. in tents, schools and churches) were set up.
- International aid provided funds and support.
- Around 1,500 people, either volunteers or the military, provided aid locally.

- Rescue workers evacuated around 700 people.
- Farmers received financial support to cover the loss of profits.
- Temporary shelter, fresh water and food were provided for evacuees.

Molten lava

Long-Term Responses

- Government agencies promoted the volcano as an attraction to restore the tourism industry.
- Barriers were built to try and control lahars.
- Over 2,000 people were moved to safer houses. Aid organisations continue to house displaced people years after the event.

- Homes and infrastructure were repaired.
- Government agencies promoted the volcano as an attraction to restore the tourism industry.
- Technology (e.g. drones) was used to further improve Iceland's volcanic monitoring systems.

Mount Merapi tourist

daydream EDUCATION

Living with Tectonic Hazards

Despite the risks associated with earthquakes or volcanic eruptions, people choose to live in areas affected by them for various reasons.

Why People Live Near Tectonic Hazards

- I'm paid to mine volcanic minerals. I need to be here for my job.
- If anything happens, I trust our earthquake-resistant buildings are strong enough to protect us.
- The soil in volcanic areas is extremely fertile, making it excellent for agriculture.
- Moving would mean leaving my friends and family, and I don't want to do that.
- Geothermal energy plants create lots of job opportunities.
- Housing is far cheaper in these areas. I can't afford to move.
- Our economy is very strong in part because tourists flock to see our volcanoes.

Risk Management

Management strategies can help to reduce the impact of tectonic hazards.

	Earthquakes	Volcanoes
Monitoring & Prediction	Seismometers, lasers and GPS receivers can detect or measure movements in the ground. Scientists can monitor the movement of tectonic plates to make predictions and provide vital warnings.	Scientists closely monitor volcanic activity such as land bulges, tremors, sulphuric gas emissions and water temperatures to make predictions. Identifying these warning signs early gives people time to evacuate.
Protection	Earthquake-resistant buildings and infrastructure can be built and existing buildings strengthened (mitigation). Nuclear power stations can use shut-down mechanisms for added protection. When an earthquake occurs, strong furniture, such as desks and tables, can be used as overhead protection.	Protecting against volcanoes is extremely difficult, and the priority is always to evacuate. Other protective measures include shutting windows and doors to block out ash and creating lava diversion channels. Also, people should avoid low-lying areas because of the risk of mudflows (lahars).
Planning	Evacuation plans should be made to get people out of danger as quickly as possible. Emergency aid supplies can be prepared in advance, and emergency services can be given specialist training. People can be educated on what to do in the event of an earthquake or eruption. Building in high-risk areas can be banned.	

23

Climate Change

Climate, the weather in an area over a long period of time, is always changing.

During the last 2.6 million years, or the Quaternary period, global temperatures have been gradually falling, with the Earth's climate alternating between glacial and interglacial states.

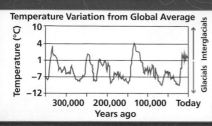

Temperature Variation from Global Average

Temperature (°C): 10, 4, 1, −7, −12

300,000 200,000 100,000 Today
Years ago

Glacials ↕ Interglacials

During the Quaternary period, glacial episodes have typically lasted 100,000 years. Interglacial periods are much shorter and typically last 10,000 years.

Average Global Temperature

Temperature (°C): 14.7, 14.5, 14.3, 14.1, 13.9, 13.7, 13.5

1880 1900 1920 1940 1960 1980 2000 2020
Year

The Earth is currently in an interglacial state, which began approximately 11,500 years ago. Over the last century, global temperatures have increased sharply, leading to global warming.

Evidence for Climate Change

There are various methods scientists can use to work out how climate has changed over time.

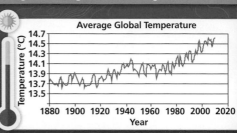

Sediment Cores
The remains of organisms in ocean sediments can be analysed to identify environmental conditions, and in turn temperatures, from the last 5 million years.

Tree Rings
A tree grows a new ring every year. In warmer, wetter years, tree rings are thicker. Therefore, tree rings can reveal evidence of temperature and weather changes over the past 10,000 years.

Ice Cores
Scientists can analyse the gas levels in ice cores to determine how temperatures have changed over 400,000 years.

Temperature Records
Since the mid-19th century, global temperatures have been measured using a thermometer. This gives accurate short-term data to track changes in temperatures.

Pollen Analysis
Pollen from plants is preserved in lake beds and bogs. Analysis of pollen can help identify plants that grew in the past and the periods and climates in which they grew.

Historical Records
Sources such as the Frost Fair drawings, farm produce audits, written descriptions and even cave paintings can reveal information about the climate in a given place and time.

daydream EDUCATION

Managing Climate Change

Climate change can have devastating effects on people and the environment. Mitigation and adaptation are two strategies that are being used to reduce the effects of climate change.

Mitigation
Mitigation strategies aim to reduce the causes of global warming by reducing the concentration of greenhouse gases in the atmosphere.

Alternative Energy Production

Alternative energy sources, such as nuclear power, hydroelectric power (HEP) and solar power, release less greenhouse gases than burning fossil fuels.

The EU's Renewable Energy Directive sets a binding target of 20% final energy consumption from renewable sources by 2020.

Carbon Capture and Storage (CCS)

Carbon capture involves capturing CO_2 released by industry or through burning fossil fuels and then storing it safely underground. This reduces the amount of CO_2 in the atmosphere.

According to the International Energy Agency (IEA), CCS can provide 20% of carbon cuts needed by 2050.

International Agreements

As part of international agreements, countries agree to common policies, such as reducing greenhouse gases by a set amount by a certain date.

The Paris Agreement (signed by over 170 countries) is one of the main agreements, although the United States withdrew in 2017.

Planting Trees

Reforestation aims to reverse deforestation by planting trees. As more trees are planted, more CO_2 is removed from the atmosphere.

The largest tropical reforestation effort in history, led by Conservation International, aims to restore 73 million trees in the Brazilian Amazon by 2023.

Adaptation
Adaptation strategies aim to limit the negative effects of climate change on humans.

Changing Agricultural Systems

Agriculture practices will need to be modified in the future to account for changing temperatures and rainfall patterns. Farmers may need to change the crops they grow or when they grow them. For example, they may need to grow more drought-resistant crops.

Managing Water Supplies

With many areas set to get drier, water needs to be managed sustainably. Water meters and water-efficient devices can be installed to encourage reduced water use. The water supply can also be increased through practices such as desalination or recycling rain water.

Adjusting to Rising Sea Levels

Sea levels have risen by over 200 mm since 1870 and are set to continue rising. Physical defences such as sea walls and barriers reduce the risk of flooding, but these are often very expensive. In LICs, homes built in high-risk areas are often raised on stilts as expensive physical defences are not an option.

Climate Change: Causes & Effects

Evidence shows that since the beginning of the Quaternary period, changes in the Earth's climate have occurred naturally. However, over the last 200 years, human factors have also contributed to climate change.

Natural Factors
There are several possible natural causes of climate change.

Orbital Changes

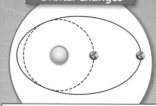

The Earth's orbit changes from circular to elliptical, which affects its distance from the Sun. When the orbit is more circular, the Earth's temperature is likely to increase, as the Earth is closer to the Sun. When the orbit is elliptical, the temperature is likely to decrease, as the Earth is further from the Sun.

Volcanic Activity

Volcanic eruptions release particles of SO_2 and CO_2 into the atmosphere. The SO_2 particles reflect the Sun's rays, reducing temperatures in the short term. Conversely, CO_2 is a greenhouse gas; it traps the Sun's heat, resulting in warmer global temperatures.

Solar Output

The Sun's solar energy output varies over time, which could result in changes to the Earth's climate. However, over the last 50 years, the Sun's energy output has declined slightly, despite the rise in global temperatures. Therefore, many people reject this theory.

Human Factors

The greenhouse effect is a naturally occurring phenomenon that insulates the Earth and keeps it warm enough to sustain life. However, it is believed that human activity increases the greenhouse effect, resulting in higher global temperatures.

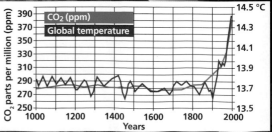

a When the Sun's solar radiation reaches the Earth's surface, most of it is absorbed, but some is reflected into the atmosphere.

b Some of this solar energy passes through the atmosphere and back into space.

c Some of it is trapped by greenhouse gases, such as methane and CO_2 in the atmosphere.

Several human activities increase the levels of greenhouse gases in the atmosphere, trapping more of the Sun's solar energy.

This graph shows the correlation between the average global temperature and the level of CO_2 in the atmosphere over time.

daydream EDUCATION

Fossil Fuels

Fossil fuels such as oil, gas and coal are burnt to generate energy for transportation, manufacturing and electricity production. However, the process of burning fossil fuels releases CO_2 into the atmosphere and is the main source of greenhouse gas emissions.

Agriculture

Agriculture, especially livestock and rice farming, produces huge amounts of the greenhouse gas methane. It is released by animals during digestion and by matter decomposed by microbes in flooded rice paddy fields.

Deforestation

Trees absorb CO_2 through photosynthesis. Therefore, clearing trees results in less CO_2 being removed from the atmosphere. This is worsened by the burning of fossil fuels, which also releases greenhouse gases into the atmosphere.

Effects of Climate Change

Climate change has a significant effect on both the environment and people.

Effects on the Environment

Warmer global temperatures will cause glaciers and ice sheets to melt, leading to rising sea levels and the loss of polar habitats.

Rising sea levels will result in low-lying coastal areas flooding more frequently or even becoming permanently submerged in water.

Many species of plants and animals are at risk of becoming extinct as their habitats are altered or damaged by climate change. For example, many of the world's coral reefs, which support a diverse range of marine life, are at risk of bleaching and destruction due to rising sea temperatures.

Warmer temperatures and higher sea levels will lead to more extreme weather events and a change in precipitation patterns.

Effects on People

As global temperatures rise, people in already hot regions will be at increased risk of developing heat-related health problems.

Many coastal areas at risk of flooding and areas that experience extremely high temperatures may become uninhabitable. This could lead to mass migration and overcrowding.

Although agriculture in some areas may benefit from warmer temperatures, many areas will become hotter and drier. This will result in drought, desertification and declining crop yields.

Drought and reduced crop yields will cause food and water shortages in many areas.

Ecosystems

Ecosystems are living communities of organisms and their physical environment. They are comprised of interconnected abiotic (non-living) and biotic (living) elements.

Food Chains & Food Webs

The biotic elements of an ecosystem interact to form food chains and food webs.

Food Chains

A food chain shows the direct transfer of energy between organisms in an ecosystem. In a food chain, organisms can be classed as producers, consumers or decomposers.

Energy	Producers	Consumers	Decomposers

The Sun is the source of all energy.

Producers (e.g. hawthorns) convert sunlight into energy to produce food.

Consumers (e.g. mice) feed on producers, other consumers or both.

Decomposers (e.g. fungi) feed on dead or decaying matter.

Food Webs

A food web is a series of interlinked food chains. The food web example below shows the interaction between producers and consumers within an ecosystem. In this example:

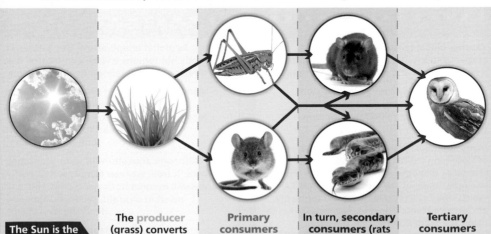

The Sun is the source of all energy.

The producer (grass) converts sunlight into food through photosynthesis.

Primary consumers (grasshoppers and mice) feed on the producer.

In turn, secondary consumers (rats and snakes) feed on the primary consumers.

Tertiary consumers (owls) can feed on all other consumers.

daydream
EDUCATION

Interdependence

All parts of an ecosystem are interdependent. This means that if one factor changes, it will affect the other organisms within the ecosystem.

The weather is hot and little rainfall occurs. → Fewer plants grow. → Less food & shelter cause grasshopper and mouse populations to shrink. → Less food causes rat and snake populations to shrink. → Less food causes the owl population to shrink.

Changes to any part of the ecosystem can cause problems for consumers further along the food chain.

Nutrient Cycles

All living organisms need nutrients from food to survive. The nutrient cycle demonstrates how minerals are stored, moved and recycled within an ecosystem.

Nutrients dissolved in rain

Tissues die (fallout)

3 Biomass (energy from plants and animals)

Rain runs off, carrying nutrients

1 Litter (dead organic matter)

Nutrients are released through decomposition

2 Soil

Plants take in nutrients through their roots

Nutrients are released from weathered rock

1 In an ecosystem, nutrients are dissolved in rainfall or stored in dead or waste matter as **litter**. Nutrients in the leaf litter will run off in rainwater, whereas others will decompose and be released into the soil.

2 Once in the **soil**, these nutrients will be added to the nutrients that have been released from weathered rock. Some of these nutrients will then be either washed out of the soil (leaching) or taken up by plants through their roots.

3 Nutrients in plants (producers) are stored in **biomass** and can be passed through food chains when they are eaten by consumers. When these producers and consumers die, the dead matter becomes litter, and the nutrient cycle begins again.

 daydream
EDUCATION

Photocopying or scanning this image is a breach of copyright law.

Global Ecosystems

As a result of differences in climate, various ecosystems called biomes have evolved throughout the world. There are **eight major biomes** on the Earth.

TDF	**Temperate Deciduous Forests**
TG	**Temperate Grasslands**
CF	**Coniferous Forests**
T	**Tundra**
TR	**Tropical Rainforests**
TrG	**Tropical Grasslands**
M	**Mediterranean**
D	**Deserts**

PACIFIC OCEAN

ATLANTIC OCEAN

Temperate Deciduous Forests (TDF)

- These forests are found mostly in mid-latitudes where rainfall occurs all year.
- There are four seasons. Summers are usually warm and winters mild.
- Deciduous trees lose their leaves in winter.
- Trees include oak, beech and maple.

Temperate Grasslands (TG)

- These regions are found between 40° and 60° north and south of the Equator.
- Summers are hot and winters cold.
- Nutrient-rich soils are well-suited for growing crops.
- Grasses include blue grama and buffalo grass.

Tropical Rainforests (TR)

- Tropical rainforests are found near the Equator.
- The weather is hot and wet year round.
- These regions have high levels of rain due to the concentrated sunlight heating the moist air.
- Trees include rubber trees and açaí trees.

Tropical Grasslands (TrG)

- Tropical grasslands are found between the Tropics.
- There are two seasons: dry and wet. However, rainfall is low (<900 mm per year).
- There are high levels of evaporation.
- Plants include red oat grass and açaí trees.

daydream EDUCATION

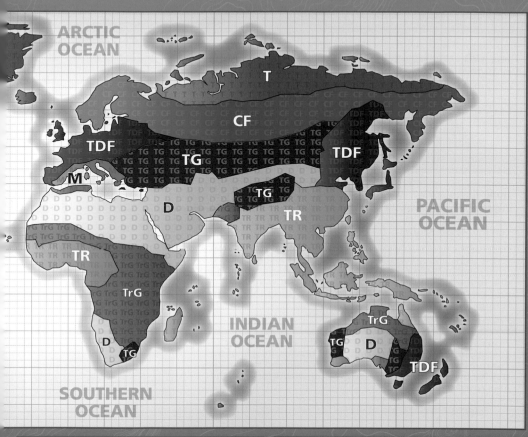

Coniferous Forests (CF)

- These regions are found between 50° and 60° north of the Equator.
- Summers are short, and winters are long and cold.
- There are high levels of precipitation, including snow in winter.
- Evergreen trees include spruce and fir.

Tundra (T)

- Tundra regions are found at high latitudes where rainfall is low.
- Summers are short, and winters are long and cold.
- The ground is generally frozen (permafrost).
- Plants include Arctic moss and bearberry.

Mediterranean (M)

- Mediterranean regions are found between 30° and 45° north and south of the Equator.
- There are two seasons: hot, dry summers and mild, wet winters.
- Semi-drought–resistant plants include olive trees, scrub and vines.

Deserts (D)

- Deserts are found between 15° and 35° north and south of the Equator.
- Days are extremely hot and nights cold.
- Rainfall levels are very low (<250 mm per year).
- Plants are sparse and include hawthorns and cacti.

Tropical Rainforests

Physical Characteristics

Tropical rainforests are found close to the Equator, where the climate is hot and humid all year round. The concentrated sunlight warms the moist air, and as it rises, it condenses to form large clouds and convectional rain. This results in high annual rainfall.

 2000–3000 mm rainfall | 25–30°C | No distinct seasons*

Some rainforests, such as the Amazon rainforest, do have a 'dry' season.

Vegetation and Soil

More than two-thirds of the world's plant species are found in tropical rainforests.

There are various layers of vegetation, including high **emergent trees** that are over 50 m tall (e.g. evergreens), mid-level **canopies** and low-level **shrubs**.

Despite the rainforest's diverse vegetation, its soil is not very fertile as heavy rain washes away nutrients. Most nutrients come from dead matter on the rainforest floor that decomposes quickly due to the hot, humid conditions. The constant warm, wet weather speeds up the nutrient cycle and ensures the growing season lasts all year.

Animals and People

Tropical rainforests are home to half of the world's animal species, including toucans, jaguars and gorillas. People of the rainforest rely on their surroundings for food and shelter. They survive by hunting, fishing, and growing plants for food and medicines.

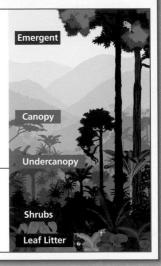

Emergent

Canopy

Undercanopy

Shrubs

Leaf Litter

Interdependence of the Ecosystem

All parts of the rainforest are interdependent. For example:

The warm, wet climate supports the growth of luxuriant vegetation.

Dense vegetation provides food and shelter for many species.

Insects and animals pollinate plants and spread seeds, enabling them to reproduce and grow elsewhere.

Trees release moisture into the atmosphere, which helps to form clouds and rain. This keeps the rainforest wet and reduces the risk of drought.

If one element in an ecosystem changes, other parts of the ecosystem will be affected. For example, deforestation has a huge impact on rainforest ecosystems; it reduces the number of trees, which results in loss of habitats, decreased transpiration and drier conditions.

Tropical rainforests have the greatest biodiversity of all the global ecosystems on Earth. Despite only covering 7% of the world's surface, they are home to over 50% of all animal and plant species.

Plant and Animal Adaptations

Plants and animals have developed special features that enable them to survive in the hot and humid rainforest environment. These features are known as adaptations.

Plant Adaptations

Poor soil, heavy rainfall and competition for sunlight mean that rainforest plants have had to adapt to compete and thrive in tropical conditions.

Smooth bark and waxy 'drip-trip' leaves help water to run off quickly, preventing damage.

Tall trees compete for sunlight. They have developed sturdy buttress roots to support their trunks as they grow.

Epiphytes are plants that have adapted to grow on other plants. They absorb minerals and water from the moist atmosphere.

Plants have shallow roots to help them draw nutrients from the soil surface before they are leached away.

Animal Adaptations

With an abundance of food, shelter and warmth, tropical rainforests have a diverse range of animals. However, with more animals comes more competition, and certain species have developed certain adaptations to help them survive.

Poison Dart Frogs	Bats	Glasswing Butterflies	Toucans

Poison dart frogs have toxic glands in their skin. Also their skin is brightly coloured to warn off predators.

Bats are nocturnal: they sleep all day and hunt at night. They do so to avoid hot temperatures and competition from other species.

Glasswing butterflies have transparent wings to help them blend in and hide from predators.

Toucans have long, curved beaks for reaching into tree holes to obtain otherwise unreachable food.

Deforestation

Deforestation is the clearing of rainforests and wooded areas. It is a big threat to many tropical rainforests.

Rate of Deforestation

It is estimated that 50% of the world's tropical rainforests have been lost to deforestation over the last 100 years.

Increased awareness of the importance of tropical rainforests has led many countries, such as Brazil, to reduce their deforestation rates. Although the global rate is decreasing, it continues to increase in some areas. For example, in Indonesia, large areas of the rainforest are being cleared to make way for palm oil plantations. Indonesia is the world's biggest producer of palm oil, and its economy relies on its production.

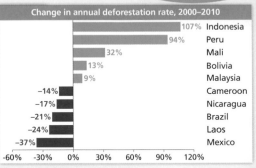

Change in annual deforestation rate, 2000–2010

Country	Change
Indonesia	107%
Peru	94%
Mali	32%
Bolivia	13%
Malaysia	9%
Cameroon	−14%
Nicaragua	−17%
Brazil	−21%
Laos	−24%
Mexico	−37%

Causes of Deforestation

There are many reasons why rainforests are being destroyed.

Overpopulation
As population grows, trees are cleared to make room for settlements.

Mining
Trees are cleared to dig for valuable minerals, such as coal and gold.

Logging
Trees are felled to harvest timber for profit. Roads must also be built to access logging sites, requiring further deforestation.

Farming & Agriculture
Trees are cleared to create space for crops and grazing livestock.

Energy Development
Forests are flooded to build dams for hydroelectric power (HEP), and areas are razed to make way for biofuel crops.

Impacts of Deforestation

Indigenous peoples have long cleared small areas of forest with little damage. However, modern large-scale deforestation has had huge environmental, economic and social impacts.

Trees remove CO_2 from the atmosphere; increased CO_2 levels contribute to the greenhouse effect and rising global temperatures. Fewer trees means fewer roots to soak up water from the soil, so more nutrients are leached. Deforestation also reduces biodiversity: plants and animals become extinct due to a lack of food and shelter.

In 1500, 6.9 million people were living in the Amazon rainforest. Only 200,000 remain there today as their homes are destroyed by deforestation. Moreover, deforestation's effects make these areas less attractive to tourists, leading to lost income. However, more jobs are being created through logging, farming and mining, and selling timber can also be very profitable.

daydream EDUCATION

Deforestation: The Amazon Rainforest

The Amazon rainforest is the largest tropical rainforest on Earth. However, a staggering one-fifth of the rainforest has been lost to deforestation since 1970.

Fact File

- The Amazon rainforest covers nearly 6 million km².
- Located in South America, it covers nine countries, including Brazil (60%), Peru (13%) and Colombia (10%).
- With over 40,000 plant species, 400 mammals, 1,300 birds and 3,000 fish, it is home to more plant and animal species than any other ecosystem on the planet.

Venezuela
Colombia
Ecuador
Peru
Brazil
Bolivia

Amazon rainforest | Deforestation
Protected area

Causes Of Deforestation

Subsistence Farming	Farmers clear areas of the forest and burn it to make room to grow crops for their families (**slash-and-burn** agriculture).
Commercial Farming	Over 70% of deforestation in the Amazon is due to commercial farming of livestock (cattle) and crops (rice, palm oil, sugar cane and coffee).
Logging	Trees are felled to sell as timber for furniture and as pulp for paper. Illegal logging is a big business in the Amazon.
Mineral Extraction	Large mines have been built in the Amazon to enable extraction of valuable minerals such as bauxite, iron ore and gold.
Energy Development	Hydroelectric (HEP) power stations have been created using dams. The Balbina reservoir alone flooded over 2,300 km² of the rainforest.
Road Building	Various roads, including the Trans-Amazonian Highway, have been built to enable greater access to the Amazon and its rich resources.
Settlements	Large areas of rainforest have been cleared to create settlements for rainforest workers, who then use some of the timber for building and fuel.
Population Growth	The Brazilian government offers land to people who move out of overcrowded cities and clear small areas for farming.

Effects Of Deforestation

Deforestation has several effects locally, nationally and globally.

Soil Erosion	Economic Development	Climate Change
When trees are removed from an area, the soil is no longer held together by tree roots. The soil erodes and its nutrients are leached, reducing soil fertility and preventing further plant growth.	The farming, mining and logging industries provide many jobs and significant income for rainforest countries, boosting their economies and helping them pay off foreign debts.	Trees in the Amazon store 20% of all the carbon in the Earth's biomass. As large portions of the rainforest are cleared, CO_2 is released into the atmosphere, adding to the greenhouse effect.

Tropical Rainforests:
Sustainable Management

The Earth's tropical rainforests must be managed sustainably if their rich natural resources and biodiversity are to be preserved for future generations.

The Value of Tropical Rainforests

Tropical rainforests are vital to people, animals, plants and the environment.

They are the world's oldest biome with the greatest biodiversity of plant and animal life.

Goods such as timber, rubber, cocoa, coffee and medicines are all sourced from tropical rainforests.

They are home to indigenous people who rely on the environment for shelter, food and medicines.

Trees absorb CO_2 from the atmosphere, limiting the greenhouse effect. They also regulate the water cycle, reducing flooding.

If rainforests are not managed sustainably, they could be wiped out completely, greatly affecting the environment both locally and globally.

Sustainable Management

There are several strategies that can be used to manage the rainforest sustainably.

Conservation and Education

Conservation is concerned with the sustainable use of natural resources. On a governmental level, this may involve protective measures, such as creating laws to stop damaging practices or setting up national parks and wildlife reserves.

Organisations such as the Nature Conservancy and WWF rely on donations to help them promote conservation through education and training programmes. They also aim to directly protect threatened areas by purchasing threatened land and creating nature reserves.

Educating people about deforestation's effects can help them understand the value of the rainforest and how it can be sustainably managed. Education is especially important for those actively involved in damaging practices and teaches people about more sustainable alternatives.

daydream EDUCATION

Debt Reduction

Most tropical rainforests are found in low-income countries (LICs) that have large debts. LICs often borrow large sums of money from high-income countries (HICs) to aid development. They also often rely upon income from activities such as logging and farming to repay their debt.

To protect rainforests, some HICs have agreed to write off LICs' debts in exchange for a guarantee to protect large areas of their rainforests. For example, in 2011, the US government agreed to convert $28.5 million of Indonesian debt into an investment to protect tropical rainforests.

Selective Logging and Replanting

Selective logging involves limiting the number and types of trees that can be felled – for example, only trees of a certain height or age. This causes less damage to the rainforest's structure and biodiversity.

Replanting involves replacing any felled trees with new trees of the same type. This helps to maintain the rainforest's long-term structure and biodiversity.

FSC
www.fsc.org
MIX
Paper from
responsible sources

Despite laws being in place to control logging, it is not always possible to enforce them because of the vastness and remoteness of rainforest areas. As a result, illegal logging is common.

Ecotourism

Ecotourism is a responsible form of tourism that supports conservation and wildlife, while also benefitting local people.

Ecotourism aims to educate visitors and minimise damage to the environment caused by tourism. It also creates employment opportunities for local people, such as work as tour guides or in hospitality.

If ecotourism programmes are managed sustainably and work to support the local community, they can positively affect an area's economy and environment.

International Agreements

International agreements can help reduce or restrict practices that damage the environment.

For example, hardwoods such as teak and mahogany have become increasingly scarce because of high demand in HICs where they are used to make wooden furniture.

To protect these woods, more than 70 nations signed the International Tropical Timber Agreement in 2006. The agreement limits the trade of tropical hardwoods. It requires hardwood timber to be felled from sustainably managed areas and marked with a legal registration number.

Hot Deserts

Physical Characteristics

Hot desert environments are found between 20° north and 30° south of the Equator, where hot, dry air sinks and causes cloud-free conditions.

Rainfall levels are low and unpredictable – it may not rain for years at a time.

Averages are less than 250 mm a year.

It is extremely hot in the day but cold at night, as there are no clouds to stop heat loss. Diurnal (daily) temperatures can range between 35-40°C in summer.

Deserts are dry and arid with little vegetation.

Covering over 9 million km², the Sahara is the largest hot desert in the world.

Vegetation and Soil

Most hot desert soil is dry and not very fertile. Due to a lack of rainfall and sparse vegetation, there is little decomposing matter to enrich the soil. The nutrients that are present decay rapidly due to high temperatures.

Only a limited number of plants, such as drought-resistant cacti, can survive the harsh desert conditions.

Animals and People

Hot deserts offer extremely challenging environments for animals and people.

Due to the hot, dry conditions, soil is poor and desert biodiversity is low. Only specially adapted animals are able to survive.

Desert people are often nomadic, meaning they keep moving in search of food and water. They grow crops where they can and rely on animals such as goats and camels for food and transport.

daydream
EDUCATION

Interdependence of the Ecosystem

Soil provides plants with nutrients and water.

Plant roots stabilise the soil, helping to prevent desertification.

The biotic (living) and abiotic (non-living) components of hot deserts are interdependent.

Plants provide animals with nutrients and water.

Animals help plants to reproduce through pollination.

The hot desert ecosystem is extremely fragile. If one component changes, it can greatly affect the other components in the ecosystem.

Climate change is making hot deserts hotter and drier. This change reduces the amount of water available for plants and animals.

Crop irrigation (artificial watering) lowers the water table underground and leaves less water available for other plants.

As the number of plants in hot deserts declines, the soil becomes less stable, and the risk of desertification increases.

Adaptations of Plants and Animals

Deserts have far less biodiversity than other global ecosystems. Plants and animals have had to develop special adaptations to survive the challenging desert conditions.

Plant Adaptations

Desert plants have had to adapt to the intense heat and dry soil.

Succulents, such as cacti and aloe, can store water in their fleshy leaves or stems. Their small, waxy leaves help to minimise water loss through transpiration. Some succulents may have toxins and sharp spines to deter thirsty animals.

Plant roots are either long and deep to reach underground water supplies or short and shallow to collect surface water when it rains.

Ephemerals, such as desert primrose, only germinate when it rains. They complete their life cycles rapidly: they grow, flower and produce seeds within a matter of weeks before dying and scattering their seeds.

Animal Adaptations

Desert animals have adapted to intense heat, a lack of water, sandy surfaces and cold nights.

Fennec Foxes

Their large ears are full of blood vessels that allow excess heat to leave their body in the day. Their fur keeps them warm during cold nights.

Camels

Camels store fat in their humps to sustain them when food and water is scarce. Their long eyelashes protect against sandstorms.

Sidewinders

Their distinctive movement helps them travel along loose, sandy surfaces and minimises bodily contact with the hot sand.

Hot Deserts: Thar Desert

Thar Desert Fact File 🔍

The Thar Desert lies partly in north-western India and partly in eastern Pakistan and covers an area of over 200,000 km². Its population of 30 million people gives it a population density greater than 80 people/km², the highest of any desert.

Dunes of Thar Desert

Challenges

Extreme temperatures and accessibility issues mean the people of the Thar Desert face many challenges.

Extreme Climate

The desert is extremely hot, with an average daytime temperature of around 46°C, though this can drop to as low as 5–10°C in winter. This heat makes outdoor work (e.g. farming) difficult. Rainfall is very low and ranges from 100 to 500 mm per year. Most rain falls during the July–September monsoon season. High evaporation rates from irrigation canals increase toxic salt in the soil, killing plants and making crop growth difficult.

Thar Desert

Inaccessibility

Road building is limited because of melting tarmac in extreme heat and little funds. Public transport is poor and relies mostly on overloaded buses. Due to the lack of roads and heavy sandstorms, some places are accessible only by camel.

Camel in Thar Desert

Water Supplies

Climate is the main cause of the Thar Desert's limited water supplies. Rainfall is unpredictable, and rivers do not flow all the time. Groundwater is the main source of water. However, this is usually found deep underground and requires a well. This water is often saline.

Development Opportunities

Though life in the Thar Desert can be challenging, the desert's location and natural resources (e.g. minerals, fossil fuels) have created a range of opportunities for future development.

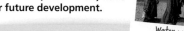
Water well

Mineral Extraction

Minerals such as gypsum, limestone and white marble are valuable building materials, and kaolin can be used to manufacture paper.

Tourism

With its exotic location and vibrant village culture, the Thar Desert attracts a growing number of tourists. Locals can earn money by selling souvenirs, acting as tour guides or offering camel rides.

Energy Production

The lignite coal and oil found in Barmer District is used to power coal-fired electricity plants in Pakistan and India. Although coal extraction remains popular, the desert's sunny climate and high winds have created opportunities to generate green energy. There is already a wind park at Jaisalmer and a solar energy plant at Bhaleri.

Farming

The Indira Gandhi Canal has provided irrigation for commercial crops such as wheat, cotton and pulses. It is also a source of drinking water. Sustainable drought-tolerant trees, such as the jujube tree, are planted to stabilise sand dunes and produce a valuable crop.

daydream
EDUCATION

Desertification

Desertification involves the degradation of arable dryland ecosystems into deserts. It occurs mainly in semi-arid areas that border hot deserts.

Causes of Desertification

Desert fringe areas are under threat from desertification because of climatic and human factors.

Climate Change

Statistics on rainfall patterns suggest that the amount and frequency of rainfall are decreasing in desert fringe areas. Decreased rainfall increases drought length and intensity, which leads to drier soils, plants dying and greater soil erosion.

Rising temperatures due to global warming also lead to increased evaporation from plants and soil. This accelerates degradation of the land.

Human Activities

Population growth and increased human activity are putting huge pressure on desert fringe areas. Increased demand for food and water means that land is being used more intensively. This eventually leads to soil erosion and desertification.

Overgrazing	Overcultivation	Removal of Fuelwood
Grazing animals strip the land of its vegetation quicker than it can grow back. Without the plant roots holding the soil together, it erodes.	Replanting crops in the same area robs the soil of vital nutrients. Crops cannot grow, and the exposed soil becomes vulnerable to erosion.	Trees are cut down for fuelwood for cooking, leaving the soil exposed and vulnerable to erosion.

Management Strategies

The risk of desertification can be reduced by using a variety of management strategies.

Water and Soil Management
Drip irrigation, rock walls (bunds) and terraces cut into slopes can help reduce water run-off and soil erosion. Crop rotation and the use of compost can help ensure soil is fertile and rich in nutrients. Drought-resistant plants, such as pigeon peas, are suited for crop growth in deserts.

Tree Planting
Trees help bind and stabilise soil to protect it from the wind and reduce erosion. They also provide shade, and their decomposing leaves add nutrients to the soil.

Use of Appropriate Technology
Affordable and sustainable new technologies can help people implement practices that reduce their impact on the land. For example, solar cookers can be used to reduce the need for fuelwood.

Cold Environments

Cold environments are harsh with low temperatures. They are found at high latitudes and high altitudes, and cover around 25% of the Earth's surface.

Physical Characteristics

There are two types of cold climate environments: polar and tundra.

Polar Environments

Polar regions are found close to the North and South poles.

There are two seasons: short, cold summers and long, freezing winters. Temperatures can reach up to 10°C in the summer, although daily averages are generally below freezing. In the winter, temperatures can drop as low as –80°C.

Precipitation levels are low (<100 mm per year). This precipitation usually falls as snow.

Tundra Environments

Tundra regions are found south of the ice cap in the northern hemisphere.

There are two seasons: short, cold summers and long, freezing winters. Temperatures rarely reach 10°C in the summer and are as low as –50°C in winter.

Precipitation levels are low (<300 mm per year). This precipitation falls as snow in winter and rain in summer.

Vegetation & Soil

The harsh conditions in polar and tundra environments result in permafrost (permanently frozen) soil, making vegetation growth difficult.

Polar regions are mostly covered in ice. Therefore, vegetation is limited to mosses, lichens and some grasses.

Plant growth is limited to the short summer months (50–60 days) when the permafrost thaws, exposing a nutrient-poor active layer of soil.

Vegetation is limited to grasses, lichens, mosses, stunted trees and low-lying shrubs.

Animals & People

Because of the extreme weather conditions in cold environments, biodiversity is low.

Animals include polar bears, penguins and walruses.

Only a small number of indigenous people inhabit the Arctic regions. They survive by fishing, herding and gathering wild plants. Scientists also stay in polar regions for research.

Animals include caribou, musk oxen and wolves.

The tundra is home to indigenous peoples, as well as workers who are employed in the oil, gas and mineral extraction industries.

daydream EDUCATION

Interdependence of the Ecosystem

The biotic (living) and abiotic (non-living) components of cold deserts are interdependent. If one component changes, it affects the other components. For example:

Indigenous peoples rely on animals for food, clothing and transport (dog sledges).

Animals help plants reproduce by spreading their seeds. Plants provide food and shelter.

Plants rely upon the snow for water and the sun for photosynthesis.

The cold desert ecosystem is extremely fragile. Therefore, any change to a single component can greatly affect other components in the ecosystem. For example:

Global warming causes permafrost to thaw, releasing greenhouse gases into the atmosphere. This causes further global warming and thawing of permafrost. The thawing of permafrost leaves the soil waterlogged, killing plants. Animals have less vegetation to feed on.

Adaptations of Plants & Animals

Plants and animals have developed special features that enable them to survive in challenging conditions. These features are known as adaptations.

Plant Adaptations

Extreme cold, strong winds, and poor soil create a hostile environment for plant growth. Adaptations help plants to overcome some of these challenges.

Shallow root systems allow many plants in cold environments to grow in the active layer above the permafrost.

Some plants, such as the pasque flower, are covered in small hairs that create a layer of insulation.

Some vegetation can grow without soil. For example, lichens can grow on rocks due to a symbiotic relationship with fungi: lichens photosynthesise and give nutrients to the fungi, and the fungi provide the structure for lichens to grow on.

Animal Adaptations

Animals in cold environments have adapted to extreme temperatures.

Elk

Elk clear snow and ice with their muzzles and hard hooves to reach the plants they must eat to survive.

Musk Oxen

Musk oxen have a coat of thick, hollow hairs that trap body heat and keep them warm.

Arctic Hares

Arctic hares are covered in thick, white fur for insulation and camouflage.

Cold Environments: Alaska, USA

Alaska Fact File

Alaska is the largest and most north-westerly state in the USA. Despite covering a huge area, it has a population of less than 750,000, including around 100,000 Inuit and Alaska Natives. Because of its cold tundra environment, most of Alaska is uninhabitable and sparsely populated. Over 40% of its population lives in the city of Anchorage, which is on the on the milder, more accessible southern coast.

Anchorage, Alaska

Challenges

Alaska's remoteness and extreme climate means that the state and its residents face many challenges.

Extreme Climate

Alaska is extremely cold, with temperatures reaching as low as −30°C in the north of the state and −10°C in the south.
Icy cold winds and blizzards create a harsh environment that inhibits farming and can pose severe health risks. In the north of the state, there can be over 60 days of non-stop darkness in the winter and over 80 days of uninterrupted sunlight in the summer.

Mountains in Alaska

Inaccessibility

Many parts of Alaska are sparsely populated because of their harsh environment and remote location. Snow and ice make roads unusable for most of the winter, and thawing in the summer often leads to mudflows and flooding. This leaves Alaska's remote settlements isolated.

Snow on roads

Buildings and Infrastructure

Raised house in Alaska

Most construction in Alaska must occur during the summer. Permafrost and summer thawing make it difficult, dangerous and expensive to build infrastructure. Buildings need strong, deep foundations to prevent subsidence in summer, when the active layer melts. Permafrost makes burying pipes and cables difficult.

The above factors combine to make living in Alaska challenging, both physically and financially. The cost of living in Anchorage, Alaska's largest city, is around 30% higher than the national average. Therefore, to attract new workers, wages must be high.

daydream
EDUCATION

Development Opportunities

Despite its cold climate and harsh environment, Alaska has used its natural resources to develop opportunities in multiple industries to generate economic growth.

Mineral Extraction

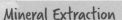

Alaska has abundant mineral resources, including copper, iron ore, silver and gold. Mining is one of Alaska's biggest industries, generating thousands of jobs and contributing billions of dollars to the economy. There is still huge potential for growth in mineral extraction. However, there is significant opposition to new mining developments because of its environmental impacts.

Oil and Gas

Alaska's waters are believed to contain more than 30% of the USA's known recoverable offshore resources. With the Trans-Alaska Pipeline System (TAPS) operating at only one-third of its capacity, there are great opportunities for development. However, extraction and transport costs are high, and like mineral extraction, many oppose development due to concerns about the environment.

Renewable Energy

Alaska's location and environment allow it to access renewable energy resources, as well as oil and gas. The steep glaciated terrain in Alaska is suited for the generation of hydroelectric power (HEP). It is Alaska's largest source of renewable energy, supplying about 21% of the state's electrical energy. Alaska's coast is also situated on the Pacific Ring of Fire, which provides opportunities for the development of geothermal power.

Fishing

With thousands of rivers, millions of lakes and an extensive coastline, there is a wealth of development opportunities for fishing in Alaska. It has some of the world's largest crab, whitefish and salmon fisheries, which are vital to the economy. However, to remain successful, Alaskan fisheries need to be managed sustainably.

Tourism

Over 2 million tourists per year visit Alaska's unique wilderness. Tourism generated $2.42 billion in 2016 alone. Its unspoilt scenery, glaciers, mountains and wildlife are a big attraction. Cruises account for over 50% of visitors and enable them to visit otherwise difficult-to-access areas.

All of the opportunities above have a significant multiplier effect on the economy, boosting government income, investment in infrastructure, and retail and service businesses.

Cold Environments: Sustainable Management

Cold environments contain fragile areas of wilderness that need to be protected for future generations.

The Value of Cold Environments

Wilderness areas are unspoilt, natural environments that have not been altered by human activity. Protection of these valuable ecological and scientific resources is vitally important.

- ✓ They provide a natural environment or 'baseline' with little influence from humans. This allows people to better recognise the effects of development.

- ✓ As home to a diverse range of plants and animals, they help to protect biodiversity.

- ✓ They contain organisms with important genetic material that can be used for research.

Wilderness areas also perform important ecosystem processes. For example, polar ice sheets reflect sunlight, which helps to regulate global temperatures.

Fragile Environments

Cold environments are fragile. If any part is altered, it can take a long time to recover and return to its original state.

For example, plant growth is extremely slow. If vegetation is damaged (e.g. from trampling or tyre tracks), regrowth can take a long time.

Also, it is extremely difficult for specially-adapted wilderness plants and animals to adjust to change. For example, the snowshoe hare relies on ice for camouflage in winter. As global temperatures rise, snow and ice begins to melt, making the hare more exposed to predators.

Management Strategies

Economic development can have disastrous effects on cold environments. However, management strategies can help balance economic development with conservation.

International Agreements	Agreements and treaties protect cold environments. For example, the 1986 commercial whaling ban has enabled some whale populations to grow. Also, the 1959 Antarctic Treaty has limited the damage caused by human activity in Antarctica.
Conservation Groups	Organisations (e.g. Greenpeace, the UN Environment Programme and the World Wide Fund for Nature) pressure governments and work with them to protect the natural environment. Some groups also protest the exploitation of the environment.
Technology	Technology can help reduce the impact of development. For example, heat from pipelines, which can melt permafrost and trigger landslides, can be elevated using stilts. Radiators can also be used to transfer heat from the pipes into the air.
Role of Governments	Governments can set aside wilderness areas for conservation, such as national parks, and put laws in place to protect cold environments, such as the Antarctic Act 2013.

UK Physical Landscapes

The UK landscape has a range of upland and lowland areas and extensive river systems.

The UK's main upland areas (more than 200 m above sea level) are found in the north and west. The main lowland areas (less than 200 m above sea level) are found in the east and south of the UK.

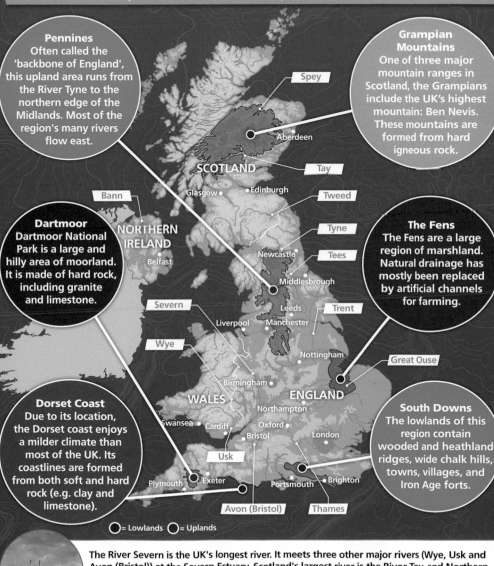

Pennines
Often called the 'backbone of England', this upland area runs from the River Tyne to the northern edge of the Midlands. Most of the region's many rivers flow east.

Grampian Mountains
One of three major mountain ranges in Scotland, the Grampians include the UK's highest mountain: Ben Nevis. These mountains are formed from hard igneous rock.

Dartmoor
Dartmoor National Park is a large and hilly area of moorland. It is made of hard rock, including granite and limestone.

The Fens
The Fens are a large region of marshland. Natural drainage has mostly been replaced by artificial channels for farming.

Dorset Coast
Due to its location, the Dorset coast enjoys a milder climate than most of the UK. Its coastlines are formed from both soft and hard rock (e.g. clay and limestone).

South Downs
The lowlands of this region contain wooded and heathland ridges, wide chalk hills, towns, villages, and Iron Age forts.

Spey
Aberdeen
SCOTLAND
Tay
Tweed
Glasgow • Edinburgh
Bann
NORTHERN IRELAND
Tyne
Belfast
Newcastle
Tees
Middlesbrough
Severn
Leeds
Trent
Liverpool • Manchester
Wye
Nottingham
Great Ouse
Birmingham
ENGLAND
WALES
Northampton
Swansea • Cardiff
Oxford
Bristol
London
Usk
Plymouth • Exeter
Portsmouth • Brighton
Avon (Bristol)
Thames

O = Lowlands   O = Uplands

The River Severn is the UK's longest river. It meets three other major rivers (Wye, Usk and Avon (Bristol)) at the Severn Estuary. Scotland's largest river is the River Tay, and Northern Ireland's longest river is the River Bann. Many of the UK's major cities are located on its main rivers. Cities found along rivers are in lowland areas.

Coastal Processes

The sea shapes the coast through various processes, including weathering, erosion, transportation and deposition.

Waves

Coastal landscapes are shaped by waves.

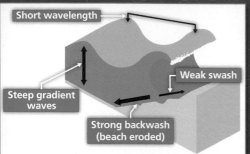

- Short wavelength
- Steep gradient waves
- Weak swash
- Strong backwash (beach eroded)

Destructive waves have a high frequency, and their backwash is stronger than their swash. This results in erosion and the removal of coastal material.

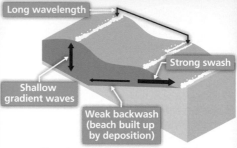

- Long wavelength
- Strong swash
- Shallow gradient waves
- Weak backwash (beach built up by deposition)

Constructive waves have a low frequency, and their swash is stronger than their backwash. This results in deposition and the build-up of coasts.

Weathering

Weathering involves the breakdown of rocks in situ (in their original place).

Mechanical Weathering

Mechanical weathering breaks down rock without altering its chemical composition.

Example: Freeze-thaw weathering

1. Water enters cracks in the rock.
2. The water freezes and expands, putting pressure on the rock.
3. The ice thaws, releasing pressure.
4. Repeated freezing and thawing causes the rock to break apart.

Chemical Weathering

Chemical weathering breaks down rock by altering its chemical composition.

Example: Hydrolysis

1. Some rocks react to water because of the minerals they contain.
2. Minerals react with the acids in water, making new chemical compounds.
3. These chemical compounds break down the rock over time.

For example, feldspar in granite reacts with water to form clay.

Mass Movement

Mass movement is the downward movement of rock, mud or soil due to gravity. It typically occurs when a lot of water is present – for example, after heavy rainfall.

Sliding

Material slides quickly downwards in a relatively straight line.

Slumping

Material slides with a rotation over a curved slip plane.

Rock Fall

Rocks break apart and fall, often as a result of freeze-thaw weathering.

daydream EDUCATION

Coastal erosion is the removal of sediment and rocks by waves. There are three main types:

Hydraulic Power	Abrasion	Attrition
As waves crash against a cliff, air trapped in the cliff's cracks is compressed. The repeated force of pressure and release widens the cracks and breaks the rock apart.	Sand, shingle and sediment are hurled against rocks by breaking waves. The rock is eventually worn down by this repeated rubbing and scraping.	Rocks and boulders transported by waves collide and break up into smaller pieces. This wears them down into smaller and more rounded fragments over time.

Transportation

Transportation is the movement of material.

Flow ⟶

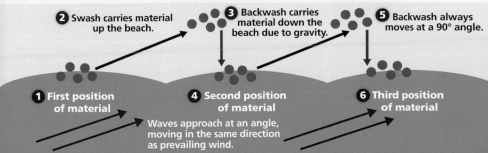

Traction	Saltation	Suspension	Solution
Large items of sediment roll along the seabed.	Smaller items of sediment bounce along the seabed.	Finer material is light enough to be carried by the water.	Minerals dissolve in the water.

Longshore drift is a process that gradually moves beach material along the coast.
The action of swash and backwash results in a zigzag movement of material.

2 Swash carries material up the beach.

3 Backwash carries material down the beach due to gravity.

5 Backwash always moves at a 90° angle.

1 First position of material

4 Second position of material

6 Third position of material

Waves approach at an angle, moving in the same direction as prevailing wind.

Deposition

Deposition occurs when the sea loses energy and drops eroded material. It is most likely to happen when:

- There are low energy waves with a weak backwash
- Waves enter sheltered areas such as bays
- Longshore drift is interrupted by structures such as groynes
- There is little wind
- Tidal water becomes trapped by spits

Beaches are formed when the level of deposition is greater than the level of erosion.
Waves that deposit more material than they erode are known as constructive waves.

Coastal Landforms

Coastal landforms are the result of physical processes that have varying effects on different structures and types of rock.

Landforms Resulting from Erosion

Headlands and Bays

Headlands and bays form where there are alternating bands of soft and hard rock.

A discordant coastline is one where bands of soft and hard rock run at right angles to the coast, so the rocks erode at different rates. The protruding bands of isolated rock are called headlands.

The formation of headlands and bays can take thousands of years.

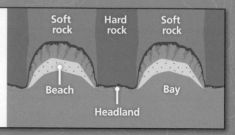

Soft rock   Hard rock   Soft rock

Beach   Bay

Headland

Wave-Cut Platforms

Effects of wind and wave power

Waves and rocks crash against the foot of a cliff face.

The base of the cliff is eroded away, leaving a wave-cut notch.

The unstable cliff collapses. With repeated erosion, the cliff retreats to form a wave-cut platform.

Caves, Arches and Stacks

Headlands are gradually eroded to form caves, arches and stacks.

1 Waves crash repeatedly into the headland, causing faults and joints to erode and develop into cracks and small caves.

2 Constant erosion causes the caves to get bigger until their back walls are eroded away completely, creating natural arches.

3 The arches widen as more rock is eroded away through weathering.

4 The arches eventually collapse, leaving an isolated pillar known as a stack. Further erosion of the stack will leave a shorter stump.

daydream
EDUCATION

Landforms Resulting from Deposition

Beaches

Beaches are the areas found between high and low tide marks. Generally formed from sand or shingle, they are the most common features of deposition found on coasts.

Sandy Beaches

- These occur where there are constructive waves.
- The **swash** (water moving up the beach) is stronger than the **backwash** (water moving back down the beach) so sediment builds up on the beach.
- Small sand particles are easily carried back down the beach by the backwash so the beaches are long and shallow.

Shingle Beaches

- These occur where there are high energy waves.
- The backwash is stronger than the swash so smaller sand particles are washed away, leaving larger sediment on the beach.
- The weak swash does not move the sediment far up the beach. This creates short and steep beaches.

Sand Dunes

Sand dunes are mounds of sand that are found behind sandy beaches. To form, they require a large, flat beach, a good supply of sand, strong winds and obstacles.

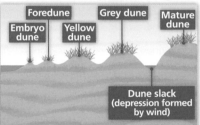

Foredune | Grey dune | Mature dune | Embryo dune | Yellow dune | Dune slack (depression formed by wind)

1. Sand is deposited by longshore drift and blown to the top of the beach by onshore winds.

2. Obstacles, such as driftwood, block sand movement, causing deposits to build over time.

3. Vegetation (e.g. marram grass) helps to stabilise and bind the sand together, creating small embryo dunes.

4. Over time, the dune migrates inland.

Bars and Spits

Spits are long stretches of sand or shingle that extend from the land. They form where the coastline suddenly changes shape (e.g. at river mouths or estuaries).

Sand and shingle are transported by longshore drift past the point where land ends. As the waves lose energy, material is deposited, forming a spit. Strong winds can cause the end of the spit to curve towards the land, creating a recurved end.

In the sheltered area behind the spit, vegetation can grow easily, and a salt marsh may form.

Bars form when a spit joins two headlands together, trapping the water in a lagoon behind it.

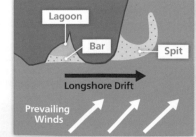

Lagoon | Bar | Spit | Longshore Drift | Prevailing Winds

Coastal Management

Coastal management aims to reduce the effects of erosion and flooding in high-risk coastal areas.

Hard Engineering

Hard engineering involves the use of man-made structures to reduce the erosive potential of waves.

Defence	Description	Advantages	Disadvantages
Sea Walls	Walls are built at the back of beaches to reflect waves back to the sea. They are usually curved to better reflect waves.	They prevent erosion but not the movement of sediment, which can affect other areas. Well-maintained walls can last for years.	They create a strong backwash, which can erode wall foundations. They are expensive to build and maintain, and can appear unsightly.
Rock Armour	Large boulders are placed along the coastline to absorb the power of waves.	It is highly effective at absorbing wave power. It is relatively cheap, quick to build and easy to maintain.	Boulders are often sourced from other locations and may appear unsightly next to the local geology.
Groynes	Concrete or wooden barriers are built at right angles to the beach to prevent longshore drift, trap sediment and absorb the power of waves.	They are relatively cheap and effective at preventing erosion. They create larger beaches, which can attract more tourists.	The restriction of the movement of sediment may simply move the problems of erosion further down the coast.
Gabions	Wire cages filled with rocks are placed at the base of cliffs to absorb wave energy.	They are cheap and easy to construct, making them a good short-term solution. They are often made from local materials.	The wire cages are ugly and can erode within 10 years. If broken, loose material can be dangerous.

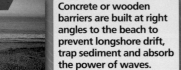

Soft Engineering

Soft engineering works with the natural environment to protect coastal areas.

Defence	Description	Advantages	Disadvantages
Beach Nourishment & Reprofiling	Sediment is either added to the beach from elsewhere or shifted from the bottom of the beach to the top.	These processes create a wider beach, which slows waves and provides greater protection from erosion and flooding.	These processes are expensive and must be repeated regularly. Beach access may be restricted during construction.
Dune Regeneration	Dunes are created or restored by adding more sand (nourishment), building fences or planting vegetation.	Dunes form an effective barrier between land and sea, and they help maintain natural habitats.	This method is expensive and requires a lot of maintenance.

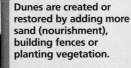

Managed retreat (or coastal realignment) allows land to become naturally flooded, creating an area of marshland or mudflats that protects inland areas. This is a cheap, natural option. However, large areas of agricultural land may be lost, and inhabitants relocated at a high cost.

daydream EDUCATION

Coastal Landforms: The Dorset Coast

The landforms of the Dorset coast have been formed over 8,000 years by the action of marine processes on the coast's unique alternating bands of hard rock and soft rock.

Fact File 🔍

- Dorset is located on the south-west coast of England.
- On its south coast the layers of rock run parallel to the coast, forming a smooth, concordant coastline.
- On its east coast, alternating layers of hard and soft rock run at right angles to the coast, forming a discordant coastline with a wide variety of landforms.

- ● Clays and Sands
- ○ Chalk
- ○ Greensands
- ● Limestones
- ● Marl

Kimmeridge Bay (Wave-cut Platforms)

The cliffs at Kimmeridge Bay have extensive wave-cut, dolerite platforms, which slope gently down to the sea.

The wave-cut platforms formed where destructive waves eroded the cliff face, causing undercutting between the high and low water marks.

Lulworth Cove (Bay)

At Lulworth Cove, waves broke through a weakness in the limestone to expose softer clays and greensand rocks.

These softer rocks eroded more quickly than the surrounding harder rocks to form this large bay.

Ballard Head (Caves, Arches and Stacks)

Ballard Head is a resistant chalk headland. Both sides of the headland were eroded by waves to form caves and arches.

Over time, some arches collapsed and formed isolated stacks several metres high. These are known as Old Harry Rocks. Further erosion caused these stacks to collapse, forming stumps.

Chesil Beach (Bar)

Chesil Beach is an example of a sand and shingle bay bar, formed by the deposition of sediment through longshore drift.

It stretches across the mouths of several bays and joins the Isle of Portland to the mainland.

daydream EDUCATION

53

Coastal Management: Holderness

Holderness Fact File

- The Holderness coast is located in north-east England.
- It is one of the fastest eroding coastlines in Europe. It loses an average of 2 metres of land to erosion each year.
- Its made up of soft boulder clay, which is very easily eroded.
- Strong prevailing winds create longshore drift which moves eroded material south along the coast. This leaves large areas of coastline exposed to erosion.

Why Are Coastal Management Schemes Needed?

English seaside resort

Large areas of the Holderness coast (e.g. Hornsea and Bridlington) are at threat from erosion, putting many businesses and homes at risk.

Coastal erosion is also threatening to damage large areas of farmland and infrastructure, including main roads and the gas terminal at Easington, which supplies 25% of the UK's gas.

What Coastal Management Schemes Are Being Used?

Various management strategies have been used to protect the Holderness coastline.

In 1991, £2 million was spent on a coastal protection scheme at Mappleton to reduce coastal erosion. Rock armour was installed to absorb wave energy, and groynes were built to prevent longshore drift and to build up the beach.

In Bridlington, a popular tourist destination, a 4.7-km long sea wall was built to protect the seafront from erosion.

Bridlington sea wall

Effects and Conflicts

Wooden groynes

- Coastal management schemes have helped protect many key areas in Holderness from erosion, including the Easington Gas Terminal, the B1242 road and the towns of Mappleton and Bridlington.
- Because of the high cost of building and maintaining coastal defences, only the most valuable locations are being protected. This leaves large areas vulnerable to damage.
- The groynes at Mappleton have prevented the movement of sediment down the coast through longshore drift. However, in doing so, this has increased the rate of erosion and subsequent loss of land further south of Mappleton.
- Unprotected areas of coastline are being eroded quicker than protected areas, causing bays and headlands to form. Headlands in unprotected areas become more exposed and increasingly difficult and costly to protect.

daydream
EDUCATION

River Valleys

The shape of river valleys change as rivers flow downstream.

The Long Profile

Upper Course

Middle Course

Lower Course

A long profile shows a river's gradient from source to mouth. A river is steepest at its source (start) and becomes gentler as it approaches its mouth (where it meets the sea).

The Cross-Profile

The processes of erosion, transportation and deposition shape river channels and valleys. The cross-profile of a river shows a simple cross-section at certain points of its course.

Cross-Profile	Features	River and Valley Characteristics
Upper course	Waterfalls, gorges, interlocking spurs, large rocks and boulders	- The river flows downhill due to gravity. This creates friction and results in lots of vertical erosion. - The river channel is narrow and shallow. - The valley is V-shaped with steep sides.
Middle course	Meanders, floodplains, smaller pebbles and rocks	- Lateral erosion increases as the river becomes less steep. - The river channel is wide and deep. - The valley is V-shaped with shallow sides.
Lower course	Meanders, oxbow lakes, floodplains, levees and fine sand particles	- A lot of lateral erosion occurs. - The river channel is very wide and deep. - The valley sides are wide and almost flat. - Deposition is most evident here.

Why does a river's velocity increase downstream despite its gradient getting shallower?

The velocity of a river is determined by more than just its gradient. The shape of its channel, the volume of water that it carries and the sediment it contains also affect its velocity.

In the upper course, a river carries a small amount of water and has a narrow, shallow and rough channel, which results in lots of friction and slows the flow of water.

Downstream, as tributary streams join the river, the volume of water increases. This combined with the wider, deeper and smoother channel (which creates less friction) increases the river's velocity.

Fluvial Processes

As a river flows along its course, it shapes the surrounding landscape through three main fluvial (river) processes.

Erosion

Erosion involves the wearing away of land. It occurs most rapidly when a river is in flood, as this is when it has the most energy.

Hydraulic Action – The force of the river compresses air trapped in cracks in the banks. The increased pressure weakens and gradually wears away the banks.

Solution – Where water is slightly acidic, it dissolves certain types of rock on the river bed and banks (e.g. limestone) and carries them as the water flows.

There are four main types of erosion.

Abrasion – Rocks carried by the river rub and scrape along the river bed and banks, wearing them down.

Attrition – Rocks carried by the river collide with each other and break into smaller pieces.

Lateral erosion occurs when riverbanks are eroded, making the river channel wider. This is most common in the middle and lower courses.

Vertical erosion occurs when the river bed is eroded, making the channel deeper. This is most common in the upper course.

Transportation

Transportation is the movement of eroded material.

River flow

Traction – Large rocks and boulders roll along the river bed.

Saltation – Smaller rocks and boulders bounce along the river bed.

Suspension – Finer, lighter material is light enough to be carried in the water.

Solution – Minerals (e.g. rock salt) dissolve and are carried along by the water.

Deposition

Deposition occurs when a river loses energy and drops eroded material (sediment).

A river will deposit its load along its course wherever its energy drops; for example, on the inside bend of a meander, in areas of shallow water and at the mouth of rivers.

When a river loses energy, the heaviest rocks and boulders are deposited first, and the lightest materials are deposited last.

daydream
EDUCATION

Rivers: Erosional Landforms

Interlocking spurs, waterfalls and gorges are all formed through processes of erosion. They are usually found in the upper course of a river.

Interlocking Spurs

In the upper course of a river, water and the material it carries cut into the river bed, creating a steep-sided **V-shaped valley**.

The river is not powerful enough to erode laterally through areas of hard rock, so it winds and bends around these rocks.

The winding path of the river creates a winding valley of **interlocking spurs**.

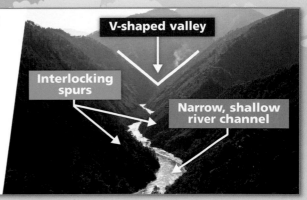

V-shaped valley

Interlocking spurs

Narrow, shallow river channel

Waterfalls and Gorges

Waterfalls form where there are rocks of varying hardness and density. Softer, less dense rock is eroded away faster than the overlying hard rock.

4

3

Hard Rock

2

Soft Rock

1

Plunge pool

Jagged rocks from collapsed ledge

1	Soft rock is eroded easily through hydraulic action and abrasion, enabling the river to cut down into the channel.
2	Over thousands of years, the river continues to erode the soft rock, and a plunge pool develops.
3	The overlying hard rock (cap rock) is undercut and left unsupported until it eventually collapses.
4	The falling hard rock causes further erosion through abrasion, and the waterfall begins to retreat upstream.

Gorges

As erosion continues, the waterfall retreats upstream, leaving a steep-sided valley downstream. This is known as a gorge.

Rivers: Erosional and Depositional Landforms

Meanders and oxbow lakes are formed through processes of erosion and deposition. They are found in the middle and lower courses of rivers.

Meanders

When a river gets nearer to the sea, large bends called meanders develop as lateral erosion occurs. Different processes occur on either side of a meander.

Deposition

Deposition takes place on the inside bend, where the river flows slowly. The shallow channel creates greater friction, which slows the river down.

Sand and shingle are deposited on the inside of the river bend, forming slip-off slopes.

Erosion and Transportation

Erosion and transportation take place on the outside bend, where the river flows fast. The deeper channel creates less friction, which enables the water to flow quickly.

Over time, erosion causes the riverbanks to be undercut and worn away, forming river cliffs.

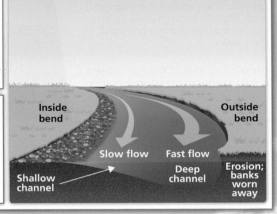

Inside bend

Outside bend

Slow flow

Fast flow

Shallow channel

Deep channel

Erosion; banks worn away

Oxbow Lakes

Oxbow lakes are formed from meanders. However, they are only found in the lower course of a river, where deposition becomes the dominant process.

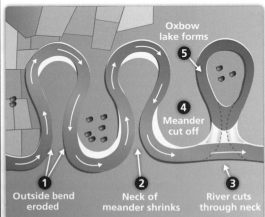

Oxbow lake forms

5

4 Meander cut off

1 Outside bend eroded

2 Neck of meander shrinks

3 River cuts through neck

1 Erosion on the outside bend of a meander causes the neck of the meander to become narrower.

2 The neck of the meander continues to narrow until the river eventually breaks through to form a new river channel.

3 The river now flows along the shortest course, bypassing the loop.

4 As sediment is deposited on the riverbanks, the meander becomes sealed off.

5 An oxbow lake forms.

Meanders and oxbow lakes may eventually dry up and form scars in the land.

daydream EDUCATION

Rivers: Depositional Landforms

Floodplains, levees and estuaries are all examples of depositional landforms. They are usually found in the middle and lower courses of a river.

Floodplains

Floodplains are wide, flat areas of land found on either side of a river. They are extremely prone to flooding.

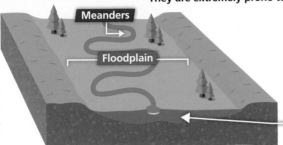

Meanders

Floodplain

When a river floods, material being carried by the river is deposited on the floodplain. Over time, this raises the height of the floodplain.

Floodplains are also made wider due to the migration of meanders.

The soil in floodplain areas is very fertile. This is due to the deposition of alluvium (silt) by the river.

Levees

Levees are naturally raised river banks that form when a river repeatedly floods and deposits sediment.

1

2

Heavier sediment

Finer, lighter sediment

3

Levees

When a river floods over its banks, the water spreads out and slows down. As it does so, it loses energy and deposits the material it has been carrying.

Heavier material is deposited first, closest to the channel. Finer, lighter material is carried further over the floodplain.

Repeated flooding and deposition forms raised levees along the edges of the channel.

Estuaries

Estuaries are found where the tidal mouth of a river meets the sea. Most were formed at the end of the Ice Age, when the sea levels rose and caused widespread coastal flooding.

Estuaries are flooded daily by the tides as they rise and fall. At high tide, the incoming tide meets the outflowing river and reduces its velocity. This causes the river to deposit its sediment (sand and silt) over the floor of the river valley.

Repeated flooding causes layers of sediment to build up over time, creating wide mudflats and salt marshes, which become exposed at low tide.

River Landscape: The River Tees

The River Tees has a range of major erosional and depositional landforms along its course.

Fact File 🔍

- The River Tees is located in north-east England.
- It is 137 km long and runs from its source at Cross Fell in the Pennine Hills to the North Sea.
- The mouth of the river is between Hartlepool and Redcar, near Middlesbrough.

North Sea

Middlesbrough

● Upper course ● Middle course ● Lower course

The Upper Course

High Force waterfall

At Cauldron Snout, vertical erosion has led to the formation of a narrow **V-shaped valley** and **interlocking spurs**. Fast-flowing rapids are prominent where the river flows over resistant whinstone.

Further downstream, England's highest waterfall, High Force (21 m), formed where less resistant limestone became exposed. The plunge pool below the waterfall has retreated over time, and a steep, narrow gorge has formed.

The Middle Course

The River Tees becomes less steep in its middle course. Lateral erosion on the outside bends of the river and deposition of material on the inside bends have led to the formation of **meanders**, **bluffs** and **alluvial banks**.

As the meanders have continually migrated, larger loops have formed, creating a flat and wide floodplain.

Meander in middle course

The Lower Course

Tees Transporter Bridge

In the lower course of the River Tees, the town of Yarm is situated on the inside of a large **meander**, which may eventually develop into an oxbow lake. Repeated flooding has also led to the formation of **levees** (raised banks) alongside the river.

Near the **estuary** (river mouth), the river slows and deposits material, forming **mudflats** and **salt marshes**, which are key wildlife habitats. One such habitat, Seal Sands, is a Special Site of Scientific Interest.

Over time, the estuary has been extensively drained and deepened for port growth and heavy industrial development.

daydream
EDUCATION

Flooding

Flooding occurs when a river's discharge exceeds its channel's volume, causing the river to overflow.

Factors Affecting Flood Risk

The speed at which precipitation reaches a river greatly affects flood risk. Any factor that causes precipitation to reach a river faster (through surface run-off) and to rapidly increase the river's discharge heightens flood risk.

Physical Causes	**Precipitation**	Prolonged, intense rainfall can saturate soil. Excess rainwater then flows to rivers as surface run-off and increases river discharge. Heavy rainfall and sudden snow melt can also cause high levels of surface run-off if the infiltration rate is too slow.
	Geology	Water cannot pass through impermeable rock, such as clay, granite and slate. Instead, water runs over the rock quickly and into the river, increasing flood risk.
	Relief	Areas with steep slopes have high levels of surface run-off because precipitation cannot infiltrate (soak through) the soil. Low-lying, flat floodplains are also highly susceptible to flooding.
Human Causes	**Land Use**	Impermeable materials and drainage systems used in urban areas increase surface run-off resulting in a greater flood risk. Deforestation reduces the amount of vegetation able to intercept rainwater.

Hydrographs

River discharge is the quantity of water that passes a given point in a river within a given time. It is measured in cumecs (m^3/s), or cubic metres per second. Hydrographs can be used to show how a river's discharge changes in response to precipitation.

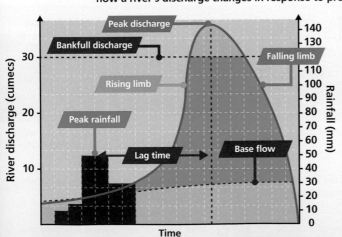

Peak Discharge
The highest level of discharge after rainfall

Peak Rainfall
The greatest rainfall during the period

Rising Limb
An increase in river discharge

Falling Limb
A decrease in river discharge

Lag Time
The time difference between peak rainfall and peak discharge

Lag time gives people time to prepare for floods. High levels of surface run-off shorten the lag time and increase peak discharge, resulting in a high flood risk. High infiltration rates increase the lag time and reduce peak discharge, lowering flood risk.

Flood Management

Different management strategies can be used to protect river landscapes from the effects of flooding.

Hard Engineering

Hard engineering involves the use of man-made structures to control the flow of a river and prevent flooding. They are an expensive, but effective flood management option.

Dams and Reservoirs

Dams are walls built across rivers to trap water, forming an artificial lake, or reservoir.

- ✔ Reservoirs store and regulate the flow of water. They can be used as a source of drinking water and to generate hydroelectric power.

- ✘ Dams are very expensive and can flood large areas of land, damaging habitats and displacing many people. They can also prevent the transportation of eroded material, reducing the fertility of farmland downstream.

River Straightening

River straightening involves cutting out meanders to create straighter, wider and deeper river channels.

- ✔ Because of less friction and the shortened river length, water flows out of an area more quickly, reducing the risk of flooding in that area.

- ✘ Flooding is more likely to occur downstream as water is carried there more quickly and the fast-flowing water causes greater erosion.

Embankments

Embankments are artificially raised banks built alongside rivers.

- ✔ The raised banks enable rivers to hold more water, protecting surrounding towns and cities.

- ✘ Embankments are expensive and can be unsightly. Devastating floods can result if an embankment fails or if the water level rises above the level of the banking.

Flood Relief Channels

Flood relief channels are used to divert water away from urban areas or to redirect water if the river level becomes too high.

- ✔ Urban areas are at less risk from flooding because water is diverted away.

- ✘ Flood relief channels are costly, and should river discharge increase significantly, they could overflow and cause severe flooding.

daydream EDUCATION

Soft Engineering

Soft engineering involves managing natural river processes to reduce the flooding risk.

Flood Warnings and Preparation

Flood alert information is issued by agencies such as the Environment Agency so people can plan and prepare for flooding.

- ☑ Warnings are cheap and give people time to evacuate and protect their homes and possessions. This can also give property owners time to reinforce their buildings to make them more flood-resistant.

- ☒ Warnings do not stop flooding and are only effective if people are aware of the warnings and take action.

Flood Plain Zoning

Flood plain zoning restricts building on flood plains and areas at risk from flooding.

- ☑ With no impermeable surfaces such as concrete or tarmac, the risk of flooding in flood plains is reduced. Also, there are no buildings that could be damaged should a flood occur.

- ☒ Flood plain zoning restricts industrial and urban development, which can increase housing shortages. It has no effect on existing high-risk urbanised areas.

Planting Trees

Trees are planted in river valleys to increase the interception and absorption of rainwater, which reduces surface run-off.

- ☑ Planting trees is a low-cost, environmentally friendly way to reduce surface run-off. It also increases natural wildlife habitats and reduces soil erosion.

- ☒ Tree planting requires a lot of space and reduces the amount of land available for farming.

River Restoration

River restoration involves removing hard engineering strategies to allow rivers to return to their natural state.

- ☑ River restoration increases water storage, reducing the risk of flooding downstream. It also makes the river more aesthetically pleasing and increases biodiversity.

- ☒ River restoration can lead to a loss in agricultural land and cause major flooding if done near high-value, built-up areas.

Flood Management: The River Tees

The River Tees is a major UK river that is at high risk of flooding. As a result, several management strategies have been implemented to reduce the risk of flooding in the surrounding area.

Fact File

- The River Tees is located in north-east England.
- It is 162 km long from its source in the Pennine Hills to the North Sea.
- The area of Teesside is an important hub for industry, and Teesport is now one of the busiest ports in the UK.

The River Tees

North Sea

Cow Green Reservoir · Darlington · Middlesbrough · Yarm

Why Are Flood Management Schemes Needed?

The steep V-shaped valleys in the upper course of the Tees are made of permeable rock, which increases run-off and causes river levels to rise quickly.

There are almost 23,500 people at risk of flooding around the Tees area. Lower Tees, Yarm and Stockton are particularly at risk from tidal floods, with Yarm experiencing severe flooding in 1995 and 2012.

Flooding at Yarm

Flood Management Strategies

Built on the inside of a large meander, Yarm is a historic market town that is prone to flooding. Since 2002, £11 million has been invested in flood management strategies to reduce the risk of flooding whilst enhancing the natural environment.

Flood Gates	Set in high reinforced concrete walls, Yarm's flood gates can be lowered to create a barrier between the town and rising waters.
Gabions	Gabions have been placed along Yarm's embankments and walls to reduce the level of erosion caused by flooding.
Flood Warnings	A Floodline Warning Direct system was set up to give the residents of Yarm (and other flood-prone areas) early flood warnings.
Flood Plain Zoning	Local authorities discourage building on low-lying land to reduce the risk of future flood damage in the town.
The Tees Barrage	The Tees Barrage, originally constructed in 1995, is now permanently kept at a high level to reduce the risk of flooding at high tide or during a storm surge.
Cow Green Reservoir	The Cow Green Reservoir, which was built in the 1970s to provide water to local industries, also helps with flood control. Future plans include a new embankment to the north of the RSPB Salthome Nature Reserve, improving flood defences and creating 30 hectares of natural habitat for wildlife.

Tees Barrage

SOCIAL ISSUES	ECONOMIC ISSUES	ENVIRONMENTAL ISSUES
Some people consider hard engineering strategies, such as the Tees Barrage, unsightly. Despite huge investment in flood defences, flooding continues to disrupt the area; for example, in Eston in 2017, flash flooding caused major travel disruptions.	Flood management is costly. For example, the Tees Barrage cost £54 million to construct. The vast number of flood defences around Teesside are also expensive to maintain.	Many people opposed the construction of the Cow Green Reservoir because they believed its construction would damage natural and man-made habitats. There are 28 environmentally designated sites in the Teesside area at risk from flooding which require protection.

daydream EDUCATION

Glacial Processes

Glaciers are huge, slow-moving masses of ice that shape landscapes through the processes of weathering, erosion, transportation and deposition.

The UK Ice Age

There have been many glacial periods over the last 2.6 million years, during which large parts of the UK were covered by huge ice sheets.

Around 20,000 years ago, ice covered most of the UK, extending as far south as the Bristol Channel.

As the Earth's climate warmed (around 10,000 years ago), the ice retreated to reveal a highly altered landscape.

Glacial Processes

Freeze-Thaw Weathering

Water flows into cracks in the rock. It then freezes and expands, widening the cracks. The ice thaws and the process repeats until the rock breaks apart.

The enormous pressure applied by a glacier's mass causes ice at its base to melt. The meltwater helps the ice to slip downhill.

Key

- Erosion
- Movement & Transportation
- Weathering
- Deposition

Rotational Slip

Glaciers often develop in hollows on mountain sides. The hollow's curved bottom allows glaciers to move in a circular motion.

The mixture of material within the glacier is known as **till**. When the ice melts, **till** is deposited and forms landforms such as moraines and drumlins. Finer material is washed away (outwash) at the glacier front.

Plucking

When moving ice meets bits of protruding rock, the pressure causes the ice to melt and refreeze on the rock's surface. As the ice starts to move, it 'plucks' out bits of rock.

Abrasion

As rock fragments embedded in the ice scrape against the rock below, the friction causes the rock to wear away. Carved out grooves called striations are left behind.

Bulldozing

As the glacier descends downhill, it pushes soil, rocks and boulders forward.

Glacial Landforms

The processes of weathering, erosion, transportation and deposition have created a wide range of unique glacial landforms.

Corries (Cwms)

Snow accumulated in hollows and formed small glaciers. Through rotational slip, the ice moved, eroding the hollows and creating large valleys with steep back walls and shallow front lips.

Pyramidal Peaks

Three or more corries developed back-to-back to form a sharp peak.

Arêtes

Two corries developed back-to-back to form a steep knife-edged ridge.

Erosional Landforms

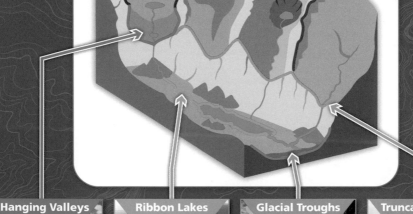

Hanging Valleys

Small tributary glaciers that flowed into larger glaciers did not erode as deeply as the larger glaciers, creating hanging valleys.

Ribbon Lakes

At the bottom of glacial troughs, glaciers eroded soft rock faster than hard rock, creating long, thin hollows and lakes.

Glacial Troughs

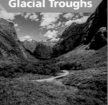

Ice moved through V-shaped valleys and eroded their sides and bottoms, forming wide, deep U-shaped valleys.

Truncated Spurs

As glaciers moved downhill with force, they eroded most obstacles. Any interlocking spurs from old river valleys were cut away, leaving cliff-like edges.

daydream EDUCATION

Depositional Landforms

When glaciers melt and retreat, they deposit **till** (unsorted clay, sand and rocks), creating depositional landforms.

Moraines

Moraines are mounds and ridges of deposited **till** left behind by a melting glacier. A moraine can be one of four types.

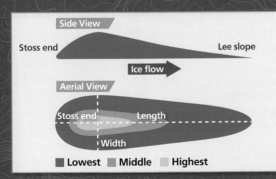

Lateral Moraines

As material is eroded from the valley sides, long mounds of deposited material form at the sides of the glaciers.

Ground Moraines

When a glacier melts, material within the glacier is deposited over a wide area of the valley floor.

Medial Moraines

A ridge of deposited material forms at the centre of the valley floor where two glaciers meet.

Terminal Moraines

Large semi-circular mounds of material bulldozed down the valley by the snout of the glacier. They mark the farthest point of glacial movement.

Drumlins

Side View

Stoss end   Lee slope

Ice flow

Aerial View

Stoss end   Length

Width

■ Lowest ■ Middle ■ Highest

Drumlins are egg-shaped, elongated hills composed of deposited material (till).

They have a steep, rounded end facing up the valley and a gently sloping, tapered end facing down the valley.

They are formed where deposited material is shaped by glaciers as they move down the valley.

Erratics

Erratics are rocks that have been transported by a glacier some distance from their original location and deposited in an area with a completely different rock type.

Erratics can look out of place and may be deposited at unusual angles.

Glacial Landforms: The Lake District

Lake District Fact File 🔍

- The Lake District is England's largest National Park, covering 2,362 km².
- The geology of the Lake District is a mix of sandstone, limestone, slate and igneous rock, such as granite.
- Over the last 500 million years geological and glacial processes have created a physical landscape of mountains and lakes, including England's highest mountain (Scafell Pike).

Features Of Upland Glacial Erosion

The 950 m Helvellyn mountain is characterised by landforms of glacial erosion.

Helvellyn

- Valley heads have corries with small lakes (tarns), including Red Tarn in the steep, armchair-shaped corrie below Hellvelyn. Rotational erosion left a shallow lip at the front of Helvellyn that, along with moraine deposits, dammed the water behind it to form a tarn.
- Brown Cove and Nethermost Cove are corries that have eroded back-to-back with Red Tarn to create the narrow, knife-edge arêtes of Striding Edge and Swirral Edge.

Features Of Lowland Glacial Erosion

The Lake District also has many features of lowland glacial erosion.

- Ice moved through pre-existing river valleys and eroded deep, U-shaped glacial troughs, including Borrowdale and Langdale, leaving high side walls and wide, flat valley floors.
- Ice eroded through interlocking spurs to form truncated spurs. Where tributary valley glaciers did not erode as deeply, this left hanging valleys such as Sourmilk Gill.

Borrowdale, Cumbria

- Many valleys have long, narrow ribbon lakes, such as Windermere, where less resistant rock was more deeply eroded or terminal moraines dammed the valley. The area's 2,000 mm rainfall helps keep the lakes full.

Features Of Glacial Deposition

Some parts of the Lake District were formed through processes of glacial deposition.

Langdale drumlins

- Ennerdale is an area characterised by glacial deposition. Large rocks, known as erratics, were carried long distances by glaciers and deposited miles from their origin by meltwater.
- 'Swarms' of egg-shaped drumlins can be spotted in the area of Langdale.

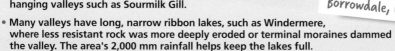

daydream
EDUCATION

Land Use in Glaciated Landscapes

Glaciated areas provide opportunities for economic activities. However, these activities also create land use conflicts that need to be managed.

£ Economic Opportunities | Conflicts with Other Land Users ✕

Tourism

- Tourism is a large source of income, providing business and job opportunities for local people.
- The beautiful landscape and lack of industry is attractive to tourists.
- The rugged hills are perfect for activities such as hiking, walking, climbing and biking.

- Increased traffic congestion and noise can upset local residents.
- Farmers are affected when dogs frighten sheep, walkers trample crops and walls are damaged.
- Increased footfall and development can damage natural habitats.

Sheep Farming

- With poor soil and steep slopes, the land is well-suited for sheep farming.
- U-shaped valley bottoms are suitable for growing some fodder crops such as hay.
- The short, wet growing season has lots of rainfall. This is good for grass, which the sheep eat.

- Conflicts can arise when farmers close pathways across their land to the public.
- Modern farm buildings can disrupt the natural landscape.
- Environmentalists may be opposed to grazing because it can destroy natural biodiversity.

Forestry

- Forestry provides employment and brings money to the economy.
- Coniferous trees are well-adapted to high rainfall and cold temperatures. Their spreading roots allow them to grow on thin, wet soils.

- Logging destroys ecosystems and disrupts wildlife.
- Newly logged areas can be unattractive and put off tourists.
- Logging areas may be closed to the public or have restricted access.

Quarrying

- Glacially eroded landscapes provide exposed rock that is easy to quarry. This rock is highly desired by many industries.
- Granite, slate and limestone are commonly quarried in glaciated areas (e.g. slate in the Lake District).

- Residents and tourists often object to the pollution caused by quarries and the large lorries that transport the quarried materials.
- Quarrying can destroy natural habitats.

Tourism in a UK Glaciated Upland Area: The Lake District

The Lake District in North West England is an example of a glaciated upland area that is used for tourism.

The Lake District Fact File

- The Lake District is England's largest national park, covering an area of 2,362 km².
- It was declared a UNESCO World Heritage Site in 2017, giving it legal protections under international treaties.
- It is home to a wide range of birds and animals, including tawny owls, badgers, foxes, bats and deer.

The Lake District

Tourist Attractions

Walking in the Lake District

The Lake District's beautiful scenery, rugged mountains (e.g. Scafell Pike) and tranquil lakes (e.g. Windermere) attract over 18 million visitors a year.

Its vast forests offer great opportunities for walking and birdwatching. Also, its cultural attractions, such as the Wordsworth Museum, and range of outdoor activities are big pull factors for tourists.

Economic Impacts

Tourism contributes over £1.46 billion a year to the local economy, supporting businesses and creating over 16,000 jobs. However, tourism also brings many challenges for residents:

- Most jobs are seasonal or part time.
- Incomes are relatively low at less than £27,000 per household.
- Due to the demand for holiday homes, house prices are high. For example, the average home in Grasmere is worth around £500,000.

Holiday cottage

Environmental Impacts

Litter on grass

Money from tourists can be used to conserve and protect areas of wildlife. However, tourism also has large-scale damaging effects on the environment:

- Walkers erode footpaths, causing damage to surrounding areas.
- Discarded litter can be hazardous to birds and animals.
- Noisy water sports on Windermere may frighten wildlife.
- Vehicles parked on verges churn up soil, destroying vegetation.

daydream EDUCATION

Social Impacts

Local residents can benefit from access to many tourist leisure facilities and some extra public transport routes in the main areas, especially in the high season. However, tourism can also make life more difficult:

- Increased traffic often blocks the narrow winding roads to the M6, particularly around tourist hotspots.
- The needs of tourists are often prioritised over those of residents.
- Commercialisation has led to traditional shops being replaced with global businesses and franchises.

Traffic jam

Sustainable Management Strategies

To minimise the negative effects of tourism, effective sustainable management strategies are key. These help conserve the environment and make life easier for local residents.

Improving Parking

- In some areas, school yards become weekend and out-of-term car parks.
- Porous pavers have helped to reinforce grass car parks.
- Controlled parking zones help to create a high turnover of vehicles.

Reducing Traffic Congestion

- Nurture Lakeland launched the Drive Less See More campaign to encourage visitors to explore the area without a car.
- The Go Lakes Travel scheme works to improve public transport, cycling and other more sustainable modes of travel.

Reducing Footpath Erosion

- Footpaths are reinforced and rebuilt by Fix the Fells, backed by the National Trust.
- The Fell Futures Apprenticeship Scheme trains people in footpath and wall maintenance.

Protecting the Environment

- Educational posters and leaflets teach tourists how to respect the area – for example, by not littering.
- At Windermere, speed limits of 10 knots were introduced, and water sports have been limited to certain zones.

Urbanisation

Urbanisation is the growth in the proportion of people living in urban environments. A growing percentage of the world's population lives in urban areas.

Rates of Urbanisation

Over 50% of the global population lives in urban areas, and this is expected to increase. Urbanisation rates differ between countries and are closely linked to wealth.

Global Urbanisation Rates, 2010–2015

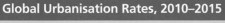

| ≥ 2% | ≥ 1% | ≥ 0% | de-urbanisation |

High-income countries (HICs) are heavily urbanised, as most of their populations already live in cities. In some HICs, people are returning to rural areas (de-urbanisation).

Newly emerging economies (NEEs) have varying urbanisation rates. In some countries, such as Brazil, the rate is slowing, but in others, such as China, the rate remains very high.

Low-income countries (LICs) are increasingly urbanising as people migrate from rural areas to towns and cities in search of jobs and better conditions.

daydream
EDUCATION

Factors Affecting Urbanisation Rates

Urbanisation occurs due to natural increases in population and rural-urban migration.

Natural increase occurs when the birth rate is higher than the death rate, increasing the population.

Birth rates increase because most migrants are young and many are likely to have children.

Death rates decrease as improved standards of living and healthcare increase life expectancies.

Rural-urban migration occurs when people move from rural areas to towns or cities.

Rural Push Factors

- Low wages and few job opportunities
- Limited access to services such as healthcare and education
- Poor living conditions
- Conflict and war
- Crop failure and famine due to natural disasters

Urban Pull Factors

- High wages and more job opportunities
- Better access to healthcare and education
- Improved standard of living
- More entertainment

Megacities

Long periods of sustained urbanisation lead to the growth of **megacities** (cities with a population of over 10 million).

There are currently over 35 megacities in the world, with more than 60% located in LICs and NEEs. Megacities in LICs include Delhi in India, and Cairo in Egypt.

Urbanisation: Mumbai, India

Mumbai Fact File

- Mumbai is located on the west coast of India.
- It is India's most populated city with over 20 million people.
- It is home to India's busiest port. Approximately 40% of India's foreign trade passes through the port.
- It is India's financial and commercial capital, and the country's richest city. The city is home to the Bombay Stock Exchange and several large transnational companies.

Mumbai, India

Causes of Urban Growth

Urban growth first began with British colonial trading and textile production. Today, **migrants** from all over India come to work in various industries, such as aerospace, engineering and medical research.

The average migrant to Mumbai is around 20 years old. Birth rates exceed death rates, contributing to natural increase.

Population (in millions) — graph showing Mumbai population growth from 1960 to 2030, y-axis 0–40, x-axis years: 1960 1970 1980 1990 2000 2010 2020 2030 Year

Opportunities

Rapid urban growth in Mumbai has seen the city embrace new social and economic opportunities.

Economic Opportunities

- The need for homes and infrastructure for the city's growing population has created opportunities for economic development.
- The planned industrial development project between Mumbai and Delhi, known as the Mumbai-Delhi Industrial Corridor, could potentially create 3 million construction and processing jobs.
- There are also opportunities for small, informal businesses in the slums (e.g. making pottery and waste recycling in Dharavi).

Pottery

Social Opportunities

Teacher and student

- Incomes in Mumbai are higher than in surrounding rural areas. There is better access to health care and education. Mumbai's literacy rate is 90%, compared to 71% in rural areas.
- Even in Dharavi, there is better access to clean, safe water than in rural India, as well as better access to electricity for domestic and business use.

daydream EDUCATION

In the newly emerging economy (NEE) of India, the megacity of Mumbai has experienced large-scale urbanisation, creating a wide range of opportunities and challenges.

Challenges

Mumbai grows by a staggering 1,500 people per day, bringing about huge challenges. Lack of housing and high rents mean that over 9 million people are forced to live in slums with Mumbai's largest slum, Dharavi, being home to over 1 million people.

Access to Water, Sanitation and Energy

- Open sewers and a lack of sanitation lead to the spread of water-borne diseases such as cholera and typhoid.
- Because of severe shortages, water is rationed from standpipes for two hours a day.
- Electricity is often sourced illegally using dangerous cable connections.

Limited Education and Health Care

- School dropout rates are high. Many students must give up their education to get a job and earn money.
- The lack of education reduces wage levels and the level of skill in the workforce.
- With high levels of disease, health services are under huge pressure.

High Unemployment and Crime

- There are not enough jobs for the rapidly increasing population.
- There is a large unskilled workforce. Many people perform informal, low-paying work under poor working conditions.
- Crime rates, especially corruption and bribery, are high.

Overcrowding and Pollution

- Roads and public transport are severely overcrowded.
- Industrial waste and traffic congestion contribute to air and water pollution.
- Poor sanitation and waste disposal lead to water pollution and the spread of disease.

Urban Planning

Indian authorities have developed strategies to try to improve the quality of life in the slums.

Mumbai Slum Electrification Project

This project aims to provide safe and reliable electricity to individual slum houses. Connection costs are 50% lower in the slums than in the main city, but daily charges can still be a barrier.

Mumbai Slum Sanitation Program

This project aims to build toilets for up to a million slum dwellers. Since 1990, authorities have built over 350 blocks containing around 7,000 toilets.

Renovation Redevelopment Plans

To help people gradually and affordably improve the structure of their homes, non-governmental-organisation provide individuals with land, grant money and architectural advice.

Urban Change in the UK: London

London Fact File

- **Location:** South-east England on the River Thames.
- **History and Growth:** Established by the Romans in around AD50. Its location at the mouth of the River Thames and close to mainland Europe helped make its port the centre for UK trade.
- **National Importance:** It is the largest and wealthiest city in the UK and home to over 10% of the UK population. It is the UK's centre for government, finance and business.
- **International Importance:** It is an international centre for media, education and culture. It is a leading global financial centre and home to the London Stock Exchange.

London's Rising Population

With a population of over 8.5 million, London is the largest city in the UK, and it is projected to continue to grow. Growth results from:

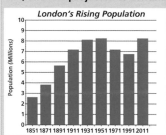

National Migration: People move to London from within the UK to study or seek employment.

International Migration: People move to London from abroad to study or work. One-third of London's population was born abroad.

Natural Increase: Most immigrants are aged between 20 and 30. This young population means that birth rates are higher than death rates.

Social and Economic Opportunities

Cultural Mix: London is the most ethnically diverse city in the UK. With a wide range of international communities (e.g. Chinatown), it offers a mix of cultures, cuisines and entertainment.

Recreation and Entertainment: London has a huge variety of sports and music venues. Historically, areas that once attracted few visitors, such as Shoreditch, are now thriving hubs of galleries, cafés and bars.

Employment: London has always had more job opportunities than the rest of the UK, especially in the service sector. Factories on the outskirts of the city also offer employment opportunities.

Transport: London has an integrated network of Tube lines, trains, and buses. Commuters can use all modes of transport under one system.

Camden Market

daydream EDUCATION

Environmental Opportunities

Urban Greening: Despite being a bustling city, London has a wealth of green spaces (e.g. Hampstead Heath). The Greener City Fund is a £9 million fund that aims to make 50% of London green by 2050 by improving green spaces and planting trees.

St James's Park

Challenges Despite its many benefits, urban change is not without its challenges.

Social and Economic Challenges

Urban Deprivation: More than a quarter of London's population lives below the poverty line. In inner city London, declining industry and poor housing conditions have led to significant deprivation.

Inequalities in Education and Employment: Students living in poorer areas often leave school with few qualifications. This leads to high levels of unemployment and low wages.

Council housing flats

Inequalities in Housing: House prices in London are rising faster than anywhere else in the UK, pricing many people out of the housing market. Affordable housing that is available is often in poor condition. For example, 60% of children in Camden live in low-income households with poor housing.

Inequalities in Health: People in deprived areas are more likely to have unhealthy lifestyles and low life expectancies. Women in Kensington can expect to live to 86, whereas those in the less wealthy borough of Dagenham have an average life expectancy of 82.

Environmental Challenges

Dereliction and Brownfield Sites: Industrial decline forced inner-city factories and buildings to close, leaving large areas polluted and derelict. Building on these brownfield sites is better for the environment than building on greenfield sites, but it is often costly to clear and decontaminate the land.

London recycling site

Waste Disposal: Around 25% of London's waste goes to landfill, and air pollution is high due to traffic congestion. Plans are in place to try and make London a zero-carbon city by 2050.

Urban Sprawl and Commuter Settlements

Urban sprawl is the growth of urban areas into surrounding rural areas. As the population grows, the demand for housing increases, causing the city to expand and 'sprawl' out.

The rate of housebuilding in London has tripled since 2013. Much of this has been along the **rural-urban fringe**, encroaching into rural areas, destroying natural habitats and harming the environment.

Commuter settlements are areas in the rural-urban fringe where people live, but work elsewhere. Near London, this has caused house prices to rocket and worsened traffic congestion.

Commuter settlements

Urban Regeneration: Stratford

Stratford in East London was an area of dereliction. Urban regeneration was needed to deal with the problem of brownfield sites, industrial outmigration, lack of jobs and extreme social inequality.

Stratford Fact File

- Stratford is located in the London Borough of Newham.
- It is in a part of the Lower Lea Valley, where the River Lea was once heavily polluted.
- After the London docks closed in the 1960s, the area deindustrialised.
- It was part of the area chosen as the site of the 2012 Olympics.

London

Stratford

Why the Area Needed Regeneration

Stratford had high levels of deprivation, with Newham having some of the highest levels of poverty in London. There were lots of brownfield sites, industrialisation and employment were in rapid decline, exam results were low and there was a significant lack of investment in the area.

Stratford was ideal as a site for regeneration for the following reasons:

- ✓ There were plenty of people looking for work.
- ✓ GCSE performance in the area was generally low and schools were in need of investment.
- ✓ With its international rail terminal, Stratford had potential for good transport links.
- ✓ The many brownfield sites were ideal for building on.

The Main Features of Stratford's Regeneration

The government used the 2012 Olympics as an engine for change in Stratford. It aimed to do the following:

Improve infrastructure. Transport improvements included new high-speed trains with a wider range of connections.

Increase affordable housing. More than 2,800 good-quality homes were built to accommodate lower-income families.

London Olympic Stadium under construction

Tackle unemployment. The International Quarter Technology Centre and Westfield complex helped to create thousands of jobs.

Boost the economy. The park brought over £9 billion of investment to the area and attracted over 8.5 million visitors over the Games period alone. This resulted in £2.1 billion of additional spending by 2016.

Improve the environment. As part of the environmentally friendly development for the 2012 Olympics, contaminated land and brownfield sites were reclaimed to create new wildlife habitats and parks.

The London Legacy Development Corporation has plans to continue improvements until 2030.

daydream
EDUCATION

Urbanisation in the UK

The population of the UK is mainly distributed around its major cities, with over 80% of people living in urban areas.

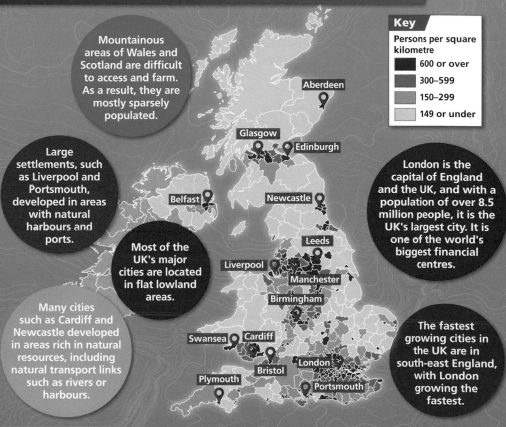

Key

Persons per square kilometre

- 600 or over
- 300–599
- 150–299
- 149 or under

Mountainous areas of Wales and Scotland are difficult to access and farm. As a result, they are mostly sparsely populated.

Large settlements, such as Liverpool and Portsmouth, developed in areas with natural harbours and ports.

London is the capital of England and the UK, and with a population of over 8.5 million people, it is the UK's largest city. It is one of the world's biggest financial centres.

Most of the UK's major cities are located in flat lowland areas.

Many cities such as Cardiff and Newcastle developed in areas rich in natural resources, including natural transport links such as rivers or harbours.

The fastest growing cities in the UK are in south-east England, with London growing the fastest.

Map labels: Aberdeen, Glasgow, Edinburgh, Belfast, Newcastle, Leeds, Liverpool, Manchester, Birmingham, Swansea, Cardiff, Plymouth, Bristol, London, Portsmouth

Urban Zones

All urban areas are different, but many develop similar characteristics and land use patterns because of economic and social factors. As a result, varying urban models have been proposed.

- Central business district (CBD)
- Factories/industry
- Low class residential
- Middle class residential
- High class residential

Burgess Model

Hoyt Model

The **Burgess Model** is one of the earliest theoretical models of urban social structures. It was later modified in the **Hoyt Model** which allowed for an outward progression of growth.

Urban Sustainability

Urban sustainability requires management of resources and transport.

The Importance of Urban Sustainability

People in urban areas have needs that must be met. However, the constant flow of **inputs** (food, water and energy) and **outputs** (waste, sewage and pollution) puts massive pressure on the environment.

Sustainable management involves using strategies to ensure that people's needs are met now, without depriving future generations.

Water Conservation

Water conservation involves the preservation, control and development of water resources and prevention of pollution.

Example: In East Village in London, water usage is just 50% of the UK average. This has been achieved through water recycling: rainwater is collected from roofs and drains, filtered by pond plants and used for toilet flushing and plant irrigation.

Energy Conservation

Energy conservation involves reducing the use of fossil fuels to save resources and reduce greenhouse gas emissions.

Example: In South London, Beddington Zero Energy Development (BedZED) has constructed insulated buildings made from thermally massive materials. These store heat during warm conditions which is then released when cool.

Waste Recycling

Recycling reduces landfill waste as well as the need for new resources to make new items. Most councils collect recyclable household items and have dumps for larger items.

Example: Greater Manchester authorities replaced 240-litre rubbish bins with new 140-litre bins in a bid to boost the city's recycling rates and save £2.4 million per year.

Creating Urban Green Spaces

Green spaces improve air quality and reduce flooding by increasing rainwater absorption. Also, people like living near green spaces: they provide a place for relaxation and exercise.

Example: One of the greenest cities in the UK, Sheffield is home to more than 250 woods, parks and gardens. There are more trees per person in Sheffield than in any other UK city!

daydream
EDUCATION

Traffic Congestion Problems

Traffic congestion and air pollution are two major problems associated with urban growth. As more people move near towns and cities, traffic congestion increases, as does air pollution.

Air pollution increases as more greenhouse gases are released into the atmosphere.

There is a higher risk of accidents, especially when the roads are busy and drivers are stressed.

Emergency vehicles may have difficulty getting through congested areas.

People commuting to work may be late due to a busy morning rush.

Traffic Congestion Solutions

Various urban transport strategies can be employed to reduce traffic congestion.

Charging more for the use of roads

Congestion charges, higher parking fees and penalties for overstaying time limits in restricted parking areas may encourage people to use public transport instead of cars.

Creating fast, efficient and reliable services, including more frequent services and designated bus lanes, will encourage people to use public transport over cars.

Improving public transport

Creating pedestrianised shopping areas

Pedestrianising main shopping areas in city centres can reduce congestion around these busy areas and make roads safer for pedestrians.

Encouraging people to drive to a large car park outside the city and take a short bus ride in can reduce the level of congestion in the city centre. This is particularly useful during busy events, such as football games and concerts.

Promoting park-and-ride services

Development

Development is the progress of a country in terms of its economic growth, use of technology and quality of life. It can be measured in various ways.

Economic Measures of Development

A country's level of development can be measured based on its **gross national income (GNI)** per head. GNI is the total income earned by a country in a year. GNI per head is value of a country's final income in a year divided by its population. It is the average income of a country's inhabitants.

GERMANY

CANADA

RUSSIA

UK

USA

MEXICO

CHINA

Key
- High-income countries (HICs)
- Newly emerging economies (NEEs)
- Low-income countries (LICs)

BRAZIL

CHAD

INDIA

AFGHANISTAN

AUSTRALIA

GNI per head, or per capita, can be used to classify countries into three broad groups.

High-Income Countries (HICs)	• HICs had a GNI per capita of at least $12,236 in 2016. • People generally have a good quality of life. Examples: UK, USA, Germany and Australia
Newly Emerging Economies (NEEs)	• NEEs are experiencing rapid economic growth. • People have an improving quality of life. Examples: Brazil, China, India and Mexico
Low-Income Countries (LICs)	• LICs had a GNI per capita of $1,005 or less in 2016. • People generally have a low quality of life. Examples: Chad, Haiti, Afghanistan and Uganda

Using only economic data to determine development has its limitations. For example, the GNI per capita of a country that has a small number of extremely rich people but lots of poor people would be misleading: the income of the rich would inflate GNI per head, giving the impression that the country is more developed than it is.

There are also lots of problems relating to data accuracy. Data can be difficult to collect, and some countries cannot or do not include all earnings in their GNI calculations. Furthermore, GNI is measured in US dollars, so data can become outdated quickly when exchange rates fluctuate.

daydream EDUCATION

Social Measures of Development

Social measures of development include birth rate, death rate and infant mortality. Generally, there is a strong correlation between social measures and economic measures.

Measure	Germany (HIC)	India (NEE)	Chad (LIC)
Birth Rate The number of births per 1,000 people each year	9.0	19.3	43.86
Death Rate The number of deaths per 1,000 people each year	11.3 (high due to ageing population)	7.3 (low due to young population)	13.2
Infant Mortality The number of deaths of infants under one year old per 1,000 births each year	3.3	36.2	76.8
People per Doctor The average number of people per doctor	250	1,380	23,000
Access to Safe Water The percentage of people who have access to clean drinking water	100%	94.1%	50%
Life Expectancy The average number of years that a person can expect to live	81	68	52
Literacy Rates The percentage of people in a population who can read and write	99%	72%	40%

Based on 2015 figures

The Human Development Index (HDI)

To ensure development is measured effectively, a variety of both economic and social measures should be used.

The HDI is a composite index that measures life expectancy, education and per capita income indicators. It ranks countries on a scale of 0 (least developed) to 1 (most developed).

		Scores
1	Norway	0.949
2	Australia	0.939
2	Switzerland	0.939
186	Chad	0.396
187	Niger	0.353
188	Central African Republic	0.352

Based on 2016 estimates for 2015 (UNDP)

The Demographic Transition Model

The Demographic Transition Model (DTM) shows how the population of a country changes over time, due to varying birth rates and death rates, and how this relates to its level of development.

The DTM suggests that identifying a country's birth rate and death rate makes it possible to determine the extent of the country's development. The DTM has five stages.

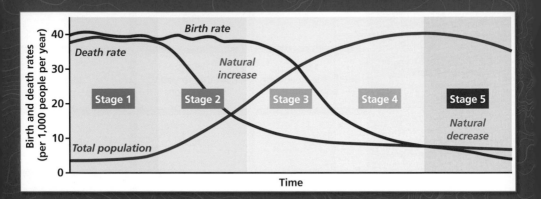

Stage 1

Birth rate:
High

Death rate:
High

Natural increase rate:
Low

The birth rate is high because of a lack of contraception, as well as to compensate for a high infant mortality rate. The death rate is also high because of poor healthcare, disease, malnutrition and inadequate sanitation.

Examples:
No countries, but may include some indigenous tribes

Stage 2

Birth rate:
High

Death rate:
Rapidly falling

Natural increase rate:
High

High birth rates continue because of a lack of contraception and a need for children to work in agriculture (the main industry). Efforts to improve healthcare and sanitation cause the death rate to fall quickly.

Examples:
Most LICs, such as Afghanistan and Mali

daydream
EDUCATION

Stage 3

Birth rate:
Rapidly falling

Death rate:
Slowly falling

Natural increase rate:
High

The birth rate falls as access to contraception and education improve and more women go to work. As subsistence living declines, there is also less need for child labour. The death rate continues to fall as healthcare and peoples' lifestyles improve.

Examples:
Most NEEs including India and Mexico

Stage 4

Birth rate:
Slowly falling

Death rate:
Low

Natural increase rate:
Low

The birth rate continues to fall because of good access to contraception. Society emphasises having a good quality of life and having material possessions as opposed to spending money on raising children. The death rate is also low because of access to good healthcare, which leads to longer life expectancies.

Examples:
HICs including the UK and Canada

Stage 5

Birth rate:
Low

Death rate:
Low

Natural increase rate:
Negative

The birth rate is low as people focus on employment and having a good quality of life. Death rates are also low as healthcare is good and life expectancies are long. However, an ageing population may result in the death rate increasing.

Examples:
HICs including Germany and Japan

Despite helping to demonstrate the link between population change and stages of development, the DTM does have its limitations. It does not account for the effects of migration, conflict, natural disasters, and social and cultural factors.

Uneven Development

There are various factors that contribute to uneven development.

Physical Factors

 The physical environment can have a major effect on a country's rate of development.

Natural Hazards

Natural hazards such as earthquakes and hurricanes can cause widespread devastation, resulting in death, injury and significant infrastructure damage.

The cost of recovery can seriously affect the population and damage the economy, leaving less money to spend on a country's development.

Climate

Countries with extremely hot or cold climates find it difficult to grow crops and produce their own food. Therefore, they must rely on imports or struggle to remain self-sufficient.

Also, people living in extreme climates often have an increased risk of illness and poor health.

Natural Resources

Countries that lack natural resources, such as timber, coal, gas and minerals, struggle to make money from exports. They may also rely on imports.

Some countries have abundant natural resources but cannot afford the infrastructure required to extract them.

Location

Location is vital for trade links, so trade can be difficult for inaccessible or landlocked countries without ports. This can make access to goods expensive.

Some countries benefit from having a location that attracts tourists, who can bring money to the economy.

Historical Factors

 Historical events and their effects can slow down a country's development.

Colonialism

In the 18th-20th centuries, European nations, such as Britain and France took control of (colonised) many parts of the world, including many African and Asian territories.

The colonial powers exploited the natural resources in these territories, with the colonies receiving little or none of the profits.

After independence, former colonies often struggled to gain political and economic stability.

Conflict

Colonial powers largely ignored cultural and ethnic differences when dividing colonies. Therefore, after independence, conflict began along many borders.

In times of conflict, money is spent on firearms, not on infrastructure and education. As people are killed or injured, and infrastructure and buildings destroyed, development is restricted.

daydream EDUCATION

There are various economic factors that can hinder growth and lead to uneven development.

Trading Primary Products

Some countries rely on the export of primary products (raw materials). However, if prices fluctuate, they may make little profit.

Countries that export manufactured products can charge more and earn greater profits, which can be used to fund development.

Debt

Some LICs may have had to borrow large sums of money. As a result, they now have high levels of debt.

In some cases, much of their income must be used to repay debts (often with added interest), reducing the amount that can be invested in development.

Trade Policies and Tariffs

Tariffs can make it extremely difficult for LICs to sell their products to other countries for a profit.

World trade often operates unfairly. Trading policies and agreements tend to favour HICs, whereas LICs are often exploited.

Consequences of Uneven Development

Uneven development has led to major consequences in terms of wealth, health and international migration.

Health

There is huge disparity in healthcare provision between HICs and LICs. For example, Africa bears 25% of cases of all the world's diseases, yet only 2% of the world's doctors.

Unclean water and poor sanitation gives rise to diseases such as cholera, and lack of medicines and vaccines leads to a higher death rate.

LICs have high infant mortality rates (e.g. Angola: 56.9 deaths per 1,000 live births) and low life expectancies (e.g. Mali: 57 years).

Wealth

Nearly 50% of the world's population lives on less than $2.50 per day.

In sub-Saharan Africa, over 40% of the population lives in extreme poverty, whereas only 2% of Iceland's population lives in extreme poverty.

Even in NEEs that have experienced recent economic growth, wealth disparity is a big problem. For example, Nigeria has one of the greatest levels of wealth inequality in the world. Nigeria's GDP grew at an average rate of 5.7% per year in the years 2006-2016. However, more than 112 million people still live in poverty due to corruption and the unequal distribution of wealth.

International Migration

Because of huge wealth disparities between countries, HICs have a greater pull factor than LICs. Therefore, skilled people in LICs often seek a better life in HICs, draining LICs of skilled workers.

In 2015, 1.38 million foreign-born individuals moved to the United States; a 2% increase from 2014. Many of these immigrants were lured by better job prospects, better healthcare and a higher quality of life.

Conflict in Africa and the Middle East has also pushed many to seek new homes, resulting in a huge increase in migration to Europe.

Reducing the Development Gap

There are various strategies that are being used in an attempt to reduce the global development gap.

Investment

Large companies can invest in LICs and NEEs to create jobs, opportunities, infrastructure and expertise. This is known as foreign direct investment (FDI).

Royal Dutch Shell employs more than 4,500 people in Nigeria – 95% of whom are Nigerian.

Microfinance Loans

Microfinance loans are provided to people in LICs who otherwise may not be able to get a loan. These loans are often used to set up businesses or to invest in and grow businesses.

The Grameen Bank in Bangladesh has provided loans to over 9 million people – 97% of whom are women.

Tourism

LICs can use their unique natural resources such as their climates, landscapes and wildlife to develop a thriving tourism industry. This can create investment and jobs for local people.

Tourism accounts for 24% of Jamaica's gross domestic product (GDP) and over 7% of its total employment.

Intermediate Technology

Intermediate technology involves the use of simple, affordable tools and machinery suitable for LICs and NEEs. Unlike high-tech alternatives, they are cheap and easy to use and maintain.

Solar box cookers in rural parts of India and Kenya produce clean and sustainable energy for domestic cooking.

Aid

Aid is the money or resources given by one country to another. It is often used to fund development projects, such as building schools or providing clean water.

The UK Government spends 0.7% of its national income on overseas development projects including those in Sierra Leone and Syria.

Industrial Development

Industrial development enables LICs and NEEs to invest in their primary industries and increase manufacturing. This increases productivity, generating more wealth for the economy. This also improves their gross national income (GNI).

In Mozambique, just six years of industrial growth (2002–2008) reduced the proportion of people living in poverty by 15%.

Debt Relief

Debt relief involves lowering the interest rates or cancelling the debt owed by struggling LICs or NEEs. This enables countries to concentrate on development and economic growth.

The World Bank has approved $76 billion in debt-reduction packages for 36 countries, including the cancellation of the Republic of Congo's $1.9 billion debt in 2010.

Fair Trade

Fair trade ensures that farmers in LICs and NEEs get a fair price for their produce, so they can provide for their families. It also aims to improve trade terms and working conditions.

More than 85% of the bananas produced in the Windward Islands are fair trade. Fair trade in Columbia has increased household income for banana farmers by an average 34%. Also, 98% of farmers said that their quality of life has improved.

Reducing the Development Gap Through Tourism: Jamaica

Fact File

- Jamaica is a Caribbean island nation with a population of around 2.8 million.
- It is an NEE with a GDP per head of $4,868.25 (2016).
- Its attractive sandy beaches, warm climate and beautiful landscapes attract tourists throughout the year. Ecotourism is also a growing industry.
- In 2016, the country attracted over 2 million tourists.

Jamaica's Development Gap

Over the last 30 years, Jamaica has suffered high levels of debt, crime, poverty and youth unemployment.

In an effort to improve its economy, the Jamaican government launched Vision 2030 in 2009. This scheme aims to make Jamaica 'the place of choice to live, work, do business, and raise families'. Some of its strategies include:

 Promoting tourism and investment in businesses and communities

 Developing new markets for health and wellness, yachting and sports tourism

 Creating more links between tourism and industries such as manufacturing and agriculture

Positive & Negative Effects Of Tourism

Tourism has both positive and negative effects on Jamaica.

Positive Effects ✔

- Tourism accounts for around 15% of Jamaica's GDP and over 50% of foreign exchange earnings.
- According to the World Travel and Tourism Council, there were around 300,000 jobs in Jamaica linked to tourism in 2016.
- Workers in other sectors also benefit from tourism. For example, local restaurants require more food from farmers.
- Higher employment means that Jamaicans have more money to spend, boosting the economy.
- Sustainable environmental tourist attractions, such as Blue Mountain National Park, attract many visitors. Income from tourism supports the management program, which includes reforestation, resource monitoring and community education.

Negative Effects ✘

- Some jobs may be temporary or seasonal, leaving many unemployed when needs change.
- Jamaica's location makes it vulnerable to extreme weather events, such as hurricanes. This makes it difficult to attract tourists during certain seasons.
- The construction of large hotels and resorts limits the farmland available to locals.
- The highest wages often go to managers from HICs, whereas locals are usually low paid. Also, large hotels and resorts owned by transnational companies (TNCs) earn most of the profits.

daydream EDUCATION

Development of an NEE: India

Fact File

India

- India is located in South Asia. It has an area of 3.3 million km².
- It has the second largest population in the world (1.3 billion).
- Once a British colony, India achieved independence in 1947.
- In 2016, India's economy was the fastest growing in the world. It currently has the world's sixth largest economy.
- India has high wealth inequality, with one in five people living in poverty. India's per capita income is around 6% that of the UK.

A Changing Industrial Structure

India's industrial structure has changed significantly as it has shifted from primary industries (e.g. agriculture) to tertiary (service) industries (e.g. IT, customer services) and experienced rapid growth.

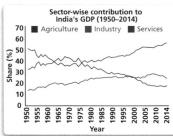

Sector-wise contribution to India's GDP (1950–2014)
■ Agriculture ■ Industry ■ Services
Share (%)
Year

The primary sector employs 50% of India's working population, but it contributes less than 20% of GDP. Jobs are often low paid and seasonal.

The secondary sector, which includes manufacturing, employs over 20% of India's working population. It provides stable jobs and contributes to the country's exports.

The tertiary sector contributes over 55% of India's GDP. Jobs are more likely to be permanent.

Transnational Corporations (TNCs)

A TNC is a company that has operations (e.g. factories, offices, research centres, shops) in more than one country. India is a popular location for many of the world's biggest TNCs because of its large pool of labour, low wages and few restrictions.

Advantages

- TNCs increase employment and tax revenues. Ford Motor Company, a foreign TNC, announced plans in 2016 to invest $195 million and create 3,000 jobs in India.
- Many TNCs invest in community projects to help development. GlaxoSmithKline's Kangaroo Mother Care project trains mothers and families in the care of low birthweight babies.
- Government and TNCs work together to improve infrastructure to accommodate large businesses. The Delhi-Mumbai Industrial Corridor will improve transport links between Delhi and Mumbai.

Disadvantages

- TNCs can create environmental and social conflict. In Kerala, Coca-Cola was accused of draining water from nearby villages and poisoning the land with waste sludge.
- TNCs may use their market power to drive down supply prices. This has been a huge problem in the tea industry. Tea prices paid by large companies have fallen dramatically, yet the prices consumers are paying continue to rise.
- Working conditions can be harsh. TNCs have been accused of using child labour in India.

daydream EDUCATION

Political & Trading Relationships

India's role in global politics and trade is growing. As it has developed, India has improved its economic and political relationships with both neighbouring countries and major global powers.

Main Imports
- Crude petroleum
- Gold and silver
- Electronic goods
- Pearls and precious stones

Main Exports
- Petroleum products
- Gems and jewellery
- Pharmaceutical products
- Transport equipment

Imports are mostly raw materials, which are processed into higher-value products and exported.

International Aid

India, like many other NEEs, has received aid from wealthier countries to support development.

Short-Term Aid	This type of aid is provided immediately after disasters. It can help fund rescue operations and emergency supplies, but it does not provide a long-term solution. **Example:** Oxfam provided 186,000 people with clean drinking water by handing out 300,000 chlorine sachets during the 2017 South Asian floods.
Long-Term Aid	This type of aid supports economic and social development over time. It aims to improve quality of life for people in NEEs and LICs. **Example:** India used to receive over £200 million in aid from the UK each year. In 2015, this ended because India was seen as sufficiently developed.
Top-Down Aid	Governments and large organisations provide aid money. The recipient government then decides which large-scale projects to spend the money on. **Example:** The Narmada Valley development project, funded by The World Bank and aid from other governments, is the largest river development scheme in India.
Bottom-Up Aid	Aid money or goods are donated directly to local people to help fund small-scale projects. This type of aid aims to improve quality of life in communities. **Example:** UNDP India has distributed more than 8,500 energy-efficient cook stoves in small communities to help save energy and reduce carbon emissions.

Impacts of Development

Economic development in India has had significant impacts on the environment and the quality of life of its population.

Environment
- Increased industrial production and energy demands have led to greater pollution. In 2017, air quality in Delhi was classed as 'very poor'.
- Development has also led to the destruction of habitats. For example, the ecosystem of the Chambal river is under threat from the actions of water hoarding, diversion, sand mining and fishing.
- Conversely, economic development has also made more money available for environmental protection. For example, in 2016, the Indian government announced plans to spend $6.2 billion on creating new forests.

Quality of Life

- Economic growth has brought more jobs and higher wages to India. It also means that there is more money to invest in healthcare and sanitation, which increases quality of life.
- There is also more money for education. More people have access to education and can gain qualifications for higher-paid jobs.
- However, many workers still suffer low wages and poor working conditions. Child labour remains a problem, especially in the cotton industry.

Economic Development in the UK

Causes of Economic Change

The UK's economy and industrial structure have changed significantly over the last 100 years.

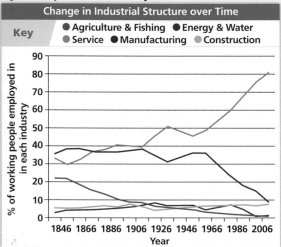

Change in Industrial Structure over Time

Key
- ● Agriculture & Fishing
- ● Service
- ● Energy & Water
- ● Manufacturing
- ● Construction

Y-axis: % of working people employed in each industry (0–90)

X-axis: Year (1846, 1866, 1886, 1906, 1926, 1946, 1966, 1986, 2006)

De-industrialisation – During the Industrial Revolution, manufacturing was the UK's leading industry. However, after declining steadily for a number of years, the 1960s saw a rapid drop in manufacturing. This has mostly been due to mechanisation, globalisation and the growth of the service industry.

Globalisation – Today, businesses often operate on a global scale, and international trade is vital for the UK's economic growth. UK companies now manufacture in NEEs, where wages and production costs are lower.

Government Policies – Government policy affects the economy. For example, decisions to invest in infrastructure and negotiate international trade deals can greatly affect growth.

The Post-Industrial Economy

The UK is now a post-industrial economy. The manufacturing industry has declined as tertiary and quaternary industries continue to grow and develop.

Information Technology — There are currently over 100,000 IT companies in the UK. The widespread use of mobile devices means companies can operate from anywhere with Internet access.

Service — The service industry is the UK's largest industry, accounting for 75% of the UK economy. Examples of this sector include health, education, retail, entertainment and hospitality.

Finance — The finance sector makes up 10% of the UK economy. London is home to internationally important financial institutions such as the Bank of England and the London Stock Exchange.

Research — Investing in research is important for long-term economic growth. UK research institutions, such as the Medical Research Council and the UK Energy Research Centre, are leaders in developing new technology.

Science and Business Parks — Science and business parks provide buildings and communications for businesses in one location. They are often on the outskirts of cities in accessible locations (e.g. near motorways) and close to universities. This helps businesses form links with a skilled workforce.

daydream EDUCATION

Impacts of Industry on the Physical Environment

Industry can negatively affect the physical environment. It can cause pollution, damage the landscape through raw mineral extraction and release hazardous chemicals into rivers.

Improved technology and greater environmental awareness has led to modern industry being more environmentally sustainable, resulting in increased efficiency and reduced pollution.

Example: Network Rail's long-term Sustainable Development Strategy plans to make efficient use of natural resources, use sustainable construction materials, and reduce, reuse or recycle as much waste as possible. By 2019, it aims to achieve a 14% reduction in carbon emissions. It is currently researching new and innovative technology to operate more sustainably in the future.

The UK Economy and Changing Rural Areas

As the UK economy changes, so do its rural areas and populations. Many people are choosing to move from urban areas to quieter and less congested rural areas (counter-urbanisation).

Area of Population Growth:
South Oxfordshire

The rural area of **South Oxfordshire** is commutable to London within around an hour.

With its easy access to the city and attractive surroundings, the population is expected to increase by over 11% by 2026. Also, the decline in local agriculture makes more land available for housing.

Area of Population Decline:
Milfield

Milfield is a small rural village in Northumberland, England, with a declining population.

In 2009, the village primary school had only seven pupils left and closed later that year. Two of the main reasons for population decline are a lack of jobs and an influx of second-home owners who push property prices up, making life unaffordable for many who live there.

Improvements and Developments in Transport

The UK is constantly improving its transport network to create better links for workers, suppliers and trading. This promotes economic growth, which benefits business and industry.

Roads	Between 2015 and 2020, the UK government plans to invest £15.2 billion in over 100 major schemes to enhance, renew and improve the road network. Also, 'smart motorways' will help manage congestion by using technology and making use of the hard shoulder to create an extra lane.
Railways	As part of a £25 billion plan, more rail lines are to be electrified, allowing for faster, quieter trains and reducing environmental damage. Also, the planned HS2 line connecting London to major northern cities will cut travel times and increase capacity.
Ports	The London Gateway is a new port on the Thames capable of handling the largest modern container ships in the world (4,000 m long). This can help boost UK trade.
Airports	The UK's largest airport, Heathrow, is reaching full capacity. To increase the number of flights, it has controversially proposed adding a new runway.

The North-South Divide

The North-South divide refers to the economic and cultural differences between Southern England and the rest of Great Britain.

North	South
Its many heavy industries were greatly affected by de-industrialisation.	It did not depend highly on heavy industry, so was less affected by de-industrialisation.
Wages are generally lower.	Wages are generally higher.
There is more unemployment.	There is less unemployment.
The standard of living is generally lower, and mortality is higher.	The standard of living is generally higher, and mortality is lower.

Reducing the North-South Divide

The gap between the North and South is increasing. In 2014, the economy of the North grew by 3%, whilst the South's grew by 6.8%. The UK government is trying to reduce this gap.

The Northern Powerhouse	Devolution	Enterprise Zones
The Northern Powerhouse is a plan to 'drive business, skills and economic growth' in the North of England through improved infrastructure, innovation and governance. It aims to link the 'core cities' of Liverpool, Leeds, Manchester, Sheffield, Hull and Newcastle.	**Devolution** involves giving more power to local authorities to make spending decisions so that they can invest money directly where it is needed locally. Scotland, Wales and Northern Ireland all have their own devolved governments.	**Enterprise Zones** have been established around the UK to encourage investment in areas of high unemployment. Businesses are offered financial incentives by the government, including reduced business rates and grants.

The UK's Place in the World

As the UK has changed and developed over the years, it has formed key links with other countries.

Trade	In 2016, the UK imported £590 billion and exported £547 billion. Imports from the EU totalled £318 billion, and exports totalled £235 billion. Outside the EU, the UK imported £42 billion from China and it exported £100 billion to the USA.
Culture	UK culture has proved popular all over the world through the success of Premier League football, music festivals such as Glastonbury, films such as James Bond, and TV shows such as The X Factor (sold to over 40 countries).
Transport	The UK is a major international transport hub. Its largest international airport, Heathrow, served 75.7 million passengers and destinations in 82 countries in 2016. The Channel Tunnel links the UK with France for trade and travel by rail.
Electronic Communications	The Internet links the UK to the rest of the world. Fibre-optic cables beneath the sea enable communication with Europe and the USA, and there are plans to lay a cable to link the UK directly to Japan.
Economic and Political Links	**The EU** is comprised of 28 countries that are part of a barrier-free trade zone. It provides valuable funds to support poorer areas of the UK. It enables EU workers to cross borders and provides UK industries with access to skilled workers. However, the UK's exit from the EU may change all of this. **The Commonwealth** is a group of 52 countries that are mostly former British colonies. All members of the Commonwealth are considered free and equal, and they share the same three aims of democracy, human rights and rule of law.

daydream
EDUCATION

Resource Management

Food, water and energy are resources essential to human development. However, there is a huge global inequality in the supply and consumption of these resources.

The Importance of Food, Water & Energy

These resources are essential for basic survival, and they contribute to people's social and economic well-being.

Food

Everybody needs a minimum daily calorie intake to live and to work. The required calories depend on factors such as age and activity level.

Too few calories can lead to malnourishment and starvation and can increase the likelihood of getting diseases.

Strong workers are vital for the economy; people need a diet with the right amount of nutrients and calories to be healthy and fit for work.

Water

Water is essential for drinking, washing, sanitation and cooking. It is also needed for industrial and manufacturing processes.

Water must be safe to drink. Unclean water can cause waterborne diseases (e.g. cholera) and death.

Water pollution can be caused by poor sanitation and by agricultural and manufacturing processes.

Energy

Energy is needed for industry, transport and domestic use.

Energy is vital for domestic uses such as cooking, lighting and heating. Electricity can be used to power water pumps and provide a clean supply of drinking water.

Energy is also vital for industrial development, which creates jobs and facilitates economic growth.

Global Inequalities in Supply and Consumption

I live in China, a newly emerging economy. We have fast-growing industries and a huge population, so our demand for resources is increasing rapidly. As our industries continue to grow, our wealth increases too. This enables us to afford more resources.

I live in the UK, a high-income country. We have high levels of development so we require lots of resources. The UK is a wealthy country that can afford the resources we need to enjoy a high standard of living. However, the distribution of wealth is not even and is getting worse.

I live in Mali, a low-income country. Although we have plenty of natural resources, our climate, unreliable water supply and poor infrastructure make it difficult to develop our economy through industry. Political unrest and conflict have also hindered development.

UK Water Patterns

Demand for water in the UK is increasing, but due to regional variations in rainfall, supply does not always meet demand.

Changing Water Demands

The increasing demand for water in the UK is due to several factors:

Domestic Use

As wealth increases, more people can afford appliances such as washing machines and dishwashers, which use a lot of water.

Agriculture

Water is vital in agriculture for irrigation. Demand for earlier seasonal food also means that crops require extra watering.

Industry

Most water extracted directly from freshwater sources is used for energy production. Water is also needed for manufacturing.

Population Growth

The UK population is expected to increase by 3.6 million over the next 10 years, which will significantly increase the demand for water.

Matching Supply and Demand

Overall, the UK has a water surplus. However, areas with the greatest population density, and the highest demand for water, do not necessarily have the greatest water supply.

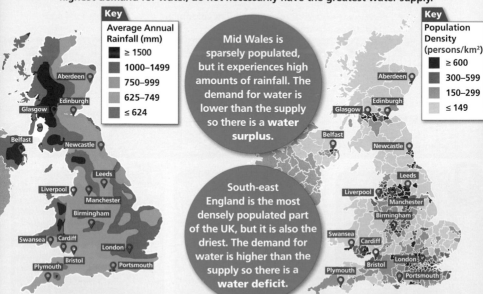

Key
Average Annual Rainfall (mm)
- ≥ 1500
- 1000–1499
- 750–999
- 625–749
- ≤ 624

Key
Population Density (persons/km²)
- ≥ 600
- 300–599
- 150–299
- ≤ 149

Mid Wales is sparsely populated, but it experiences high amounts of rainfall. The demand for water is lower than the supply so there is a **water surplus**.

South-east England is the most densely populated part of the UK, but it is also the driest. The demand for water is higher than the supply so there is a **water deficit**.

daydream EDUCATION

Water Transfer

Water transfer schemes are being used to resolve the UK's supply and demand problem. Under these schemes, water is transported from areas of surplus to areas of deficit.

The Kielder Water Scheme is a regional transfer system that allows water from Kielder Reservoir in the north-west (an area of water surplus) to be released into the Rivers Tyne, Derwent, Wear and Tees so it can be redistributed to areas of water deficit.

As well as being very expensive, water transfer can cause other problems, including:

Dams can disrupt ecosystems, for example, by blocking migrating wildlife.	Communities can be displaced when dams and reservoirs are built.	Moving water to another area can sometimes cause water insecurity in the source area.

Water Quality and Pollution Management

Over 70% of the UK's water is considered polluted or of poor quality. Causes of pollution include:

Agriculture	Chemicals such as nitrates from fertilisers and pesticides can be washed into rivers.
Industry	Industrial developments may leak pollutants and chemicals into rivers.
Oil	Oil pollution caused by spills, shipping or run-off from industry does not dissolve in water. Instead, a thick layer of oil remains on the water's surface.
Sewage	Raw sewage that contains harmful bacteria is often pumped into rivers and seas.
Litter	People may dump litter such as food packaging into rivers.

The effects of water pollution can be catastrophic. Toxins and pollutants can destroy ecosystems by poisoning wildlife and marine life. The bacteria in sewage can also result in the spread of diseases.

The following management strategies are being used to manage the UK's water quality:

Legislation

Various laws restrict the amount and type of waste that farmers and industry can put into rivers. Water suppliers are also subject to strict water quality regulations.

Water Treatment

Water treatment plants filter polluted or poor-quality water. The water is treated to kill harmful bacteria and make it safe to drink.

Education

People continue to be educated about the damage caused by littering in rivers and how to dispose of waste properly.

Investment in Infrastructure

New sewage works and improved piping infrastructure is helping to improve water quality and reduce the amount of water wastage.

UK Energy Resources

The changing demand and provision of energy in the UK has created various opportunities and challenges.

Changing Demand for Fuel in the UK

Traditionally, the UK's energy mix has consisted mainly of the fossil fuels coal, gas and oil. Nuclear power has also contributed a significant amount of energy since the 1990s.

However, fossil fuel reserves are declining, and efforts are being made to reduce greenhouse gas emissions. As such, a big shift from fossil fuels to renewable energy sources, such as wind and solar power, is occurring.

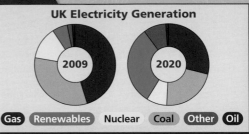

UK Electricity Generation

2009   2020

Gas   Renewables   Nuclear   Coal   Other   Oil

The UK government aims to have 30% of its energy mix made up of renewable energy by 2020.

The UK's Supplies of Coal, Gas and Oil

Coal is no longer the UK's main source of energy. Since the discovery of the North Sea gas reserves in the 1980s and increased pressure to reduce CO_2 emissions, coal production has decreased dramatically. Production is set to decline further with the last remaining coal-fired power stations due to close by 2025.

The UK has natural gas and oil reserves in the North Sea. However, these supplies are rapidly running out, forcing the UK to look at alternative energy resources. One possible resource is shale gas reserves, but to access this gas, the controversial process of fracking is being considered.

Economic and Environmental Issues

The energy sector created £24 billion in economic value and supported over 700,000 jobs during 2016. However, the exploitation of energy sources can cause various issues.

Economic Issues

The initial set-up of renewable energy resources and nuclear energy are very expensive.

Fossil fuels will become more expensive as they become scarcer and harder to extract.

Renewable energy sources are not as reliable as fossil fuels.

Nuclear power is risky, and the storing and transporting of dangerous nuclear waste is extremely expensive.

Environmental Issues

Many people believe that fracking for shale gas can cause pollution and small earthquakes.

When burned, fossil fuels release CO_2 which contributes to the greenhouse effect.

Hydroelectric power (HEP) requires dams to be built, which can destroy ecosystems.

Some people believe that wind farms and power stations spoil the natural landscape.

daydream EDUCATION

UK Food Patterns

The changing demand and provision of food in the UK has created various opportunities and challenges.

Changing Demand for Food in the UK

Historically, people ate seasonal, locally produced foods. Foods were eaten according to the seasons in which they were grown – for example, strawberries in summer and parsnips in winter.

A rise in demand for seasonal foods all year round has led to an increase in food imports. Today, almost 50% of food in UK supermarkets is imported from overseas.

Higher incomes, more varied diets and increased immigration have also led to more demand for high-value organic foods and exotic foods produced in LICs. For example, £145.6 million worth of avocados were bought in UK supermarkets in 2015, a 31% increase on the previous year.

> I want to be able to have my favourite berry smoothies all year round. In winter, my local supermarket has strawberries from Egypt.

> I appreciate high-value foods such as good-quality Costa Rican coffee beans and different spices from Asia for cooking.

> I worry about eating crops sprayed with pesticide and meat that has been fed antibiotics, so I'm prepared to pay more for organic foods.

The UK's Carbon Footprint

The huge increase in food imports into the UK has significantly increased its carbon footprint, or the total amount of greenhouse gases produced to support human activities. Each year in the UK, food travels around 30 billion km before it is consumed.

CO_2 is also released when food is grown, processed and packaged. Therefore, an increase in the demand for food has also led to an increase in CO_2 emissions.

To reduce the UK's carbon footprint, campaigns such as 'Buy British' have been launched to encourage people to buy locally sourced produce. Many schools take part in campaigns (e.g. Heinz 'Grow Your Own') to help children learn how to grow fruit and vegetables.

Agribusiness

Agribusiness is the application of business skills to agriculture. Farms are treated like industrial businesses, producing large amounts of food as efficiently as possible to reduce costs. This has several impacts on the local environment and the economy.

- Hedgerows are removed to create larger farms, reducing biodiversity.
- Manual labour is replaced by machinery, leading to job losses and greater greenhouse gas emissions.
- Chemical pesticides and fertilisers increase pollution and kill wildlife.

Global Water Demands

The global demand for water is increasing. However, there are huge variances in its availability and consumption.

Water Security

Water security is the reliable availability of an acceptable quantity and quality of water for sustaining health, livelihoods and socio-economic development.

Global Patterns of Water Surplus and Deficit

Water surplus is when clean water supply exceeds demand, resulting in water security.

This generally occurs in areas that have high rainfall and a low population density.

Water deficit is when demand for clean water exceeds supply, resulting in water insecurity. This generally occurs in areas that have low rainfall and a high population density.

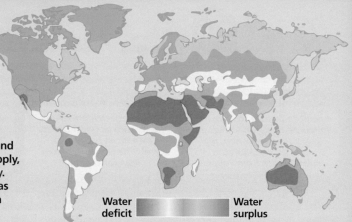

Water deficit — Water surplus

Water stress occurs when the demand for clean water exceeds the amount available during a certain period or when poor quality restricts its use.

The Rise in Global Water Demand

There are two main reasons why the demand for water is rising globally:

Economic Development

- Industry and energy production put huge strains on the water supply. For example, water is needed in agriculture for crop irrigation and in manufacturing for production and cooling machinery.

- As people earn more money, living and hygiene standards improve. As a result, more water is used for washing machines, dishwashers, flushing toilets and showers.

Population Growth

- As the global population continues to grow, an increasing number of people will need water for drinking, washing and domestic use.

- To feed the growing population, food production is increasing. However, agriculture uses vast amounts of water (e.g. for livestock and to irrigate crops), putting huge strains on the water supply.

daydream
EDUCATION

Water Insecurity

Water insecurity is a lack of access to an acceptable amount of clean water to maintain good health, livelihoods and earnings.

Factors Affecting Water Availability

Climate

Climate is the biggest factor affecting water availability. Areas with low precipitation are likely to suffer from water insecurity, especially if they are hot as lots of water is lost through evaporation. Climate change is also making the weather more unpredictable with many arid areas getting drier and hotter.

Geology

Water is unable to soak through hard, impermeable rock (e.g. granite). Instead, it flows over the rock surface into rivers, lakes, and reservoirs, which are easy to access. Conversely, water soaks into permeable rock (e.g. sandstone), sometimes forming underground stores called aquifers. These are not easy to access but can increase water availability in dry areas.

Pollution

Pollution reduces the amount of clean water available for human use. It is a particular problem in industrial areas that rely on non-renewable energy and that generate high levels of waste.

Over-Abstraction

Water can be abstracted from a source quicker than it can be replenished. This can lead to surface water and groundwater stores drying up.

Poverty

In LICs and NEEs, many people cannot afford to pay water providers for clean water. Many people have no option but to get their water from communal wells and pipes or rivers.

Limited Infrastructure

Poor or lacking infrastructure can affect water availability, limiting supply and access. Even in the UK, almost 20% of the public water supply is lost each year through leakage.

Impacts of Water Insecurity   Water insecurity has many negative impacts:

Disease & Pollution	When water is scarce, people may resort to drinking untreated or polluted water, which can give rise to waterborne diseases such as cholera. Chemicals from agriculture and manufacturing can also lead to poisoning.
Food Production	Irrigation is vital to commercial agriculture. An insufficient water supply can reduce crop yield and hinder livestock farming. The resulting drop in food production can lead to malnutrition and starvation.
Industrial Output	Industry relies heavily upon water for manufacturing, cooling and hydroelectric power. Water scarcity can lead to drops in production and dependence on expensive imports, greatly harming the economy.
Conflict	Water insecurity can lead to conflict, especially where multiple countries share supplies. For example, a dam built by one country to improve its water supply could reduce the water supply of countries downstream.

Increasing Water Supply

Over 1 billion people worldwide lack access to clean, safe water. However, there are various strategies available that can increase the water supply.

Diverting Supplies and Increasing Storage

Water can be diverted from areas of water surplus to areas of water deficit using water transfer schemes. Water is usually transferred through canals and water pipes. Also, existing river channels can be dredged (deepened) to increase capacity.

Water can be stored in tanks, aquifers or reservoirs for use in times when there is a water deficit.

However, water transfer is not without its drawbacks. It is very expensive and can disrupt ecosystems and kill wildlife.

 In the US South-West, huge volumes of water are transferred over 300 km through canals, pumping stations and tunnels from the Colorado River Basin to California. Here, the water is used mainly for irrigation and to replenish the public water supply in cities such as Los Angeles.

Dams and Reservoirs

A dam is a barrier built across a river. It traps water behind it to form an artificial lake, or reservoir.

A surplus of water builds up in reservoirs after prolonged, intense rainfall. This provides a large supply of freshwater during times of water deficit.

Dams and reservoirs can be used to generate hydroelectric power (HEP). However, dams are expensive to construct and maintain. Reservoirs also flood agricultural land, disrupt ecosystems and reduce soil fertility downstream, creating conflict with farmers.

 The Kielder Water Reservoir in Northumberland was built in 1982 (at a cost of £167 million) to supply water to the industries in north-east England. It also generates hydroelectric power.

Desalination

Desalination is the process of removing minerals from saltwater (e.g. from the sea or tidal rivers) to make it suitable for drinking or irrigation.

Desalination is mostly used in wealthy Middle Eastern countries such as Saudi Arabia. However, other countries, including the UK, also have plants for use in times of drought.

Desalination is an extremely expensive process. It requires a huge amount of energy to desalinate just one litre of water.

 The Ras Al-Khair Power and Desalination Plant in Saudi Arabia is the biggest desalination plant in the world. It is capable of producing over 700 million litres of water per day.

 daydream EDUCATION

Increasing Water Supply: China

RUSSIA
MONGOLIA
CHINA — Yellow River — Beijing, Tianjin
Danjiangkou, Shanghai
Yangtze River
INDIA

● Central ● Eastern ● Western

Fact File

- Northern China is an area of water insecurity. Its dry climate means that there is a limited supply of water. However, its large population, agriculture and industry mean that demand for water is high.

- To help alleviate the problem, the Chinese government is constructing a water transfer project to move water from the more humid south to the drier north.

How the Water Transfer Scheme Works

China's South-to-North Water Transfer Project is a network of canals and tunnels designed to transfer 44.8 billion cubic metres of water from the humid south to the arid north of the country.

Transfer will occur via three canal systems: the **Central**, the **Eastern** and the **Western**. Two of these systems, the Central and the Eastern, have already been completed.

Advantages and Disadvantages of the Scheme

China's water transfer scheme has both advantages and disadvantages.

Advantages ✔

- Large water supplies are provided to areas of water insecurity. It is estimated that 100 million people have benefitted from water transfer in the north.

- Industry uses large amounts of water. Increasing water supply supports China's economic development and generates more wealth for the country.

- Agriculture requires large amounts of water for irrigation. Increasing water supply allows more crops to be grown for food.

- By 2050, the water transfer project is expected to reach its capacity and be able to transfer 44.8 billion cubic metres of water per year.

Disadvantages ✘

- The scheme is expected to cost more than $60 billion.

- Communities have been displaced, farmland destroyed and natural habitats damaged to make way for large reservoirs, such as the Danjiangkou Reservoir.

- The completed project will mostly supply urban areas so people in rural areas will have little to no access. The project is also very expensive, so many people in urban areas will not be able to afford to access it.

- Water transfer to the north is creating water scarcity in the south. Major lakes along the Yangtze River are drying up.

daydream EDUCATION

Sustainable Water Supply

The Earth's water supply must be managed sustainably to ensure the sufficient supply of clean water for future generations.

Water Conservation

Water conservation is concerned with using less water.

At a household level, people can:

- Shower instead of bathing, and shower less frequently or for a shorter time
- Reduce their use of washing machines and other appliances that use lots of water
- Use more efficient appliances

Houses can also be fitted with water meters, so people are charged for their actual water usage. This can also discourage excessive water usage.

At a national level, the water infrastructure can be improved to reduce leaking. Almost 20% of the water supply for homes is lost through leaks.

In agriculture, farmers can switch to more efficient forms of irrigation (e.g. drip irrigation).

As well as being the biggest user of water, industry is often the biggest polluter. Controlling pollution from industrial processes can help conserve freshwater.

Groundwater Management

Groundwater management is concerned with the sustainable use of groundwater resources.

Groundwater stores, such as aquifers, are at risk from pollution and over-abstraction.

Pollution can be minimised by imposing fines on industries that leak waste into water systems. Also, farmers can be encouraged to use fewer harmful fertilisers.

Extraction can be monitored regularly to prevent over-abstraction.

Governments can impose laws limiting the amount of groundwater extraction. However, laws are not always easy to enforce, especially if stores are shared by multiple countries, and wells in LICs are largely unregulated.

Groundwater can also be artificially replenished or recharged.

Recycling

Once water has been used, it can be treated and used again. This reduces the need to extract more water from natural resources.

Recycled water can be used for irrigation, industry, flushing toilets and even washing.

Treating recycled water in sewage plants removes harmful bacteria and makes it safe to drink.

'Grey' Water

'Grey' water is relatively clean waste water from washing machines, baths, showers and sinks. It also includes rainwater collected in water butts.

This water is recycled without first being treated. It is clean enough for use in toilet flushing or for watering gardens. However, it is not suitable for drinking.

daydream
EDUCATION

Global Energy Demands

The global demand for energy resources is increasing. However, there are huge variances in energy production and consumption.

Energy Security

Energy security is access to an uninterrupted supply of energy at an affordable price to support economic and social progress.

Global Distribution of Energy Supply and Demand

Energy surplus is when energy supply exceeds demand, resulting in energy security.

Energy deficit is when demand for energy exceeds supply, resulting in energy insecurity.

An increasing number of countries face an energy gap: they are unable to produce sufficient energy from their own resources to meet rising demand.

Energy Used per Person (Btu)

- OVER 250
- 250 150
- 149 75
- 74 25
- UNDER 25

HICs consume around 50% of the world's energy, but they are some of the world's biggest energy producers. Most people in HICs have access to affordable energy.

Russia has the world's largest natural gas reserves: around 25% of the world's supplies.

Energy consumption in NEEs is increasing as industries develop and people can afford more technology.

Due to its economic growth, China was responsible for 87% of the growth in global coal consumption in 2011.

LICs often have few resources or cannot afford to exploit those that they have, so energy production is low. Also, with less development, demand is low.

Haiti has huge potential for renewable energy but lacks the wealth to develop it. The country relies on imported fossil fuels.

The Rise in Global Energy Consumption

The global consumption of energy is increasing. There are three main reasons for this:

Economic Development

NEEs such as China and India continue to develop. Along with HICs, they require more energy for technology, manufacturing and transport. Also as people become wealthier, they can afford more consumer goods, which require more energy.

Population Growth

With the global population expected to reach around 8.6 billion by 2030, more energy will be needed to meet the increased demand. People need energy for heating, cooking, technology, transport and lighting.

Technology

Technological development has led to increased demand for products that require energy. Also, increasing wealth enables more people to afford technological items, such as computers, mobile phones, cars and tablets.

Energy Insecurity

Energy insecurity is a lack of access to an uninterrupted supply of energy at an affordable price. It occurs when demand exceeds supply.

Factors Affecting Energy Supply

Physical Factors

Fossil fuels are only found in areas with suitable geology. However, some reserves may be difficult to access and/or expensive to extract.

Some areas that are hard to access or have harsh climates make fuel extraction difficult (e.g. coal in Amazonia, and the Arctic oil reserves).

Many renewable energy resources, such as wind and solar power, are also limited by climate.

Cost of Exploitation & Production

As fossil fuels become more scarce and harder to extract, their costs will increase.

Energy prices are volatile. When a resource is in high demand or limited supply, its value increases, making it more expensive.

Some countries have plenty of resources but lack the money to extract them.

The infrastructure for alternative renewable energy production can be costly.

Technology

As technology improves, new ways of extracting resources are being discovered (e.g. fracking for shale gas), which help to increase energy supply.

Some countries cannot afford the technology required to extract resources (e.g. oil in Angola).

Political Factors

International conflict can disrupt energy supply, particularly in countries that rely on imported energy. Similarly, civil wars can disrupt production and a country's ability to export.

International agreements to reduce greenhouse gas emissions encourage countries to limit the use of fossil fuels and to seek renewable energy sources.

Impacts of Energy Insecurity

Destroying Natural Habitats	As fossil fuels become scarcer, countries will be forced to extract resources from environmentally sensitive areas such as the Amazon Rainforest. Searching for fossil fuels also destroys environmentally sensitive areas.
Economic Costs	Countries, especially those that rely on imports, may not have enough energy supply to meet demand. This affects individuals, businesses and industrial production and can damage the economy.
Environmental Costs	An increase in biofuel use may result in woodland being cleared to grow the crops and trees needed to produce biofuels. Renewable energy sources, such as wind farms and hydroelectric reservoirs, can spoil landscapes and ecosystems.
Food Production	Because food production requires vast amounts of energy, energy insecurity could lead to food shortages and famine. Growing crops for biofuels also reduces the land available for growing food.
Potential for Conflict	Energy insecurity can cause conflict in areas where energy is not evenly distributed. Conflict may also arise between countries competing for resources. For example, Russia and Ukraine have an ongoing dispute over gas.

daydream
EDUCATION

Increasing Energy Supply

As the global demand for energy increases, more strategies are needed to increase the energy supply.

Renewable Energy

Renewable energy sources are a good option for increasing the energy supply because they do not run out. However, each source has its associated advantages and disadvantages.

	Use	Advantage	Disadvantage
Biomass	Organic materials, such as animal waste, wood or crops, are burned for energy or processed into biofuel.	Biomass is affordable and renewable if resources are replaced (e.g. trees are replanted).	Burning biomass releases CO_2. Using wood for fuel can lead to deforestation.
Wind	Wind turbines convert the kinetic energy in the wind to power electric generators.	Wind power produces no greenhouse gases. Once turbines have been set up, wind is a cheap source of energy.	Set-up costs are high. Some people consider turbines an eyesore and they also create noise pollution.
Hydroelectric Power (HEP)	Dams are used to trap and control water. As water is released, its kinetic energy is used to turn electric turbines.	Once infrastructure has been set up, HEP produces energy cheaply. Reservoirs provide a water supply during shortages.	Set-up costs are high. Also, when dams are built, habitats are often destroyed and people displaced.
Tidal	Currents and changes in tidal water levels are used to turn turbines and produce electricity.	Tides are guaranteed and predictable, and they produce no greenhouse gases.	Energy cannot be produced all day. Tidal barrages can disrupt ecosystems.
Geothermal	Heat from within the Earth is used to generate electricity.	Geothermal energy is a cheap energy source.	Power can only be harnessed from tectonically active areas.
Wave	Electricity is generated when waves turn turbines in the sea.	Wave power produces no greenhouse gases. It is well-suited to coastal areas.	It is costly to set up and produces little energy when the sea is calm.
Solar	Solar panels are used to convert the Sun's energy into electricity.	Once solar panels have been set up, solar energy is cheap. It produces no greenhouse gases.	No electricity is generated when there is no sunlight. Panels are expensive.

Non-Renewable Energy

Fossil Fuels - To increase energy supply, modern power stations can re-use wasted heat or burn biomass as they generate electricity. New technologies can be used to exploit resources that were once too difficult to obtain – for example, fracking to reach shale gas.

Nuclear Power - Used uranium rods can be re-used to make the most of nuclear power. However, nuclear waste is extremely dangerous and must be safely stored for thousands of years. Any accidents from nuclear plants can have disastrous effects.

daydream
EDUCATION

Increasing Energy Supply: Fracking

What is Fracking?

Fracking (hydraulic fracturing) is used to extract oil and natural gas trapped in shale rock deep underground.

1. A well is drilled vertically until it reaches the shale. The well is then drilled horizontally along the shale formation.

2. The well is reinforced with concrete and steel.

3. Water, sand and chemicals are pumped into the well at high pressure.

4. The pressure creates small cracks (fissures) in the shale, which releases any gas stored within it.

5. The liquid is pumped out of the well. The sand remains to keep the cracks open, enabling the gas to be piped to the surface.

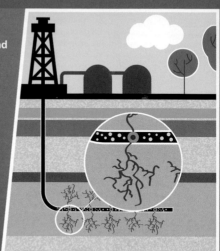

Advantages and Disadvantages

Like all methods of energy supply, fracking has its own set of advantages and disadvantages.

✔ Advantages

- It is estimated that fracking could create around 64,000 jobs in the UK.

- The UK has large shale gas reserves, particularly in Northern England. These could significantly increase the UK's energy production and reduce the risk of energy insecurity.

- Gas obtained by fracking is far cheaper than the natural gas that the UK currently imports.

- Fracking has significantly reduced gas prices in the USA and could do the same in the UK.

- Shale gas releases CO_2 when burned. However, it releases less than other fossil fuels. For example, energy produced from fracked shale gas releases only half of the CO_2 emissions that are released from coal.

✘ Disadvantages

- Fracking may cause groundwater pollution; some of the chemicals used are toxic to the environment, as well as to humans.

- Shale gas is a non-renewable energy source. Although fracking may improve the UK's energy security in the short term, it is not a long-term solution.

- Fracking uses a large amount of water, putting strain on water supplies.

- Fracking can trigger minor earthquakes. In 2011, two small earthquakes affected Blackpool near a drilling site.

- It is estimated that investment in fracking could require around £33 billion.

daydream
EDUCATION

Sustainable Energy Supply

The changing demand for and provision of energy in the UK has created various opportunities and challenges.

Individual Energy Use and Carbon Footprints

A person's carbon footprint is a measurement of the amount of greenhouse gases (e.g. carbon and methane) released into the atmosphere by the individual's activities.

> *I'm trying to reduce my carbon footprint by eating local, seasonal food to reduce my food miles.*

> *I've reduced my carbon footprint by cycling to work instead of using my car.*

> *I've installed solar panels on my house to reduce my use of fossil fuels. It has saved me money!*

Energy Conservation

Home & Workplace

- Installing double- or triple-glazed windows and insulating walls and roofs can help to contain heat within buildings and reduce energy wastage.
- Natural light should be used where possible. However, where artificial light is needed, use energy-efficient lightbulbs that use 25–85% less energy than traditional light bulbs.
- Installing technologies like solar panels and wind turbines enables homes and workplaces to generate free electricity.

Transport

All of the following actions will help reduce energy consumption and greenhouse gas emissions:

- Using public transport instead of private cars
- Reducing air travel by using alternative methods of transport
- Switching to small, efficient electric or hybrid cars

Demand Reduction

Demand for energy can be reduced by encouraging individuals and businesses to use less energy. Workplace campaigns such as Carbon Trust Empower educate people on how to do this.

Governments can also reduce demand by increasing taxes on inefficient energy use and improving the provision of public transport.

Efficient Technology

- New technology increases the efficiency of machinery and engines so that they require less energy.
- Household electrical appliances are designed to be more efficient in response to government regulations.
- Some power stations use combined heat and power (CHP) processes to make the most of the fuel they use. For example, wasted heat generated by gas turbines can be used to boil water and drive a steam turbine, which generates additional electricity.

Global Food Demands

Global demand for food is increasing. However, there are huge variances in its availability and consumption.

Food Security

According to the UN's Food and Agriculture Organization (FAO):

'Food security is when all people, at all times, have...access to sufficient, safe and nutritious food that meets their dietary needs...for an active and healthy life.'

Global Food Supply and Calorie Intake

There is enough food produced worldwide for every person to eat a nutritious diet. However, the global distribution of food is uneven; almost 800 million people do not have enough food to lead a healthy active life. This map shows average calorie consumption by country.

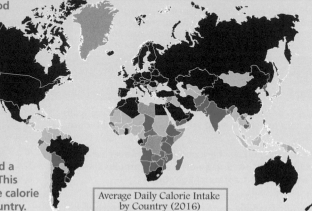

Average Daily Calorie Intake by Country (2016)

Average Daily Calories

- OVER 3,000
- 3,000 2,500
- 2,500 2,000
- UNDER 2,000
- NO DATA

HICs

People in HICs have food security. HICs often have a surplus of food, as they can produce their own food or pay to import it from other countries. People have varied diets, comprising meat, fish, grains, dairy and fats.

NEEs

Many NEEs have extreme wealth inequality. As a result, many people are often malnourished and have food insecurity. However, people's diets are becoming more varied as their wealth increases.

LICs

People in LICs have food insecurity. LICs often have a food deficit as they cannot produce enough food or afford to import food. People's diets are often limited to cereals and tubers, which can leave many malnourished and starving.

Reasons for Increased Food Consumption

Population Growth

The global population is increasing rapidly, with the UN predicting that the population will grow to 11.2 billion by 2100. To meet growing consumption demands, more food will be required.

Economic Development

People in countries that are experiencing rapid economic growth have more wealth and can afford to eat more food and a greater variety of it. Changing lifestyles in these countries also means that people are demanding convenience foods, which are often higher in calories.

Technological developments have enabled greater food production at a lower price, so people can afford to buy and eat more food.

 daydream EDUCATION

Factors Affecting Food Supply

Food supply is affected by various physical and human factors.

Climate

Some countries have climates that are not suited to farming or growing sufficient crops. Natural disasters such as drought and flooding can kill crops and livestock.

Pests and Diseases

Pests, particularly insects such as locusts, can consume an entire crop. Diseases such as foot-and-mouth can wipe out whole herds of cattle or sheep.

Water Stress

Water is vital for crops and livestock. Farming is difficult in areas where water is scarce because of excessive use or climate change.

Technology

Food production can be increased by investing in new technology and machinery, improved crop storage and genetically modified, drought-resistant plants.

Conflict

Conflict can destroy farmland and force people to flee their homes, leaving them without stable food sources. Also, destroyed transport links can prevent food being transported or received.

Poverty

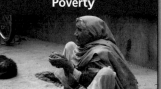

People who cannot afford land must instead buy their food, which can be expensive. Farmers who cannot afford pesticides or fertilisers are at risk of a lower crop yield.

Impacts of Food Insecurity

Food insecurity occurs when people are unable to access nutritious, affordable food. This creates a range of negative impacts.

Famine	Famine is a widespread, serious shortage of food that can lead to starvation and even death.
Undernutrition	Undernourishment occurs when people do not get enough nutrients to stay healthy, weakening their immune system. It can cause development problems in children and lead to the birth of underweight babies.
Soil Erosion	When demand for food is high, farmers face pressure to produce more food. As a result, they may try to grow too many crops, leaving the soil infertile and exposed. Overgrazing and deforestation also cause soil erosion.
Rising Prices	When demand for food increases, so do food prices. In times of food insecurity, poor people struggle to afford food and may starve or become undernourished.
Social Unrest	Food insecurity can cause great anxiety and anger among people. Growing fears about food could lead to riots, protests and even wars, which further disrupt farming and worsen shortages.

Increasing Food Supply

As the global population and demand for food continue to increase, new strategies to increase food supply are needed.

Irrigation

Irrigation involves supplying water to land to help crops and plants grow. Irrigation can increase or maintain crop yields when water supply is low or unreliable, such as in arid and semi-arid climates.

There are various types of irrigation that can be used, including:

Drip Irrigation	Sprinklers	Gravity Flow
Water is dripped from holes in pipes directly onto the soil.	Water is sprayed across fields.	Troughs are dug to divert water to where it is needed.

Aeroponics and Hydroponics

Aeroponics and **hydroponics** involve growing plants in a controlled environment without soil. They use far less water than traditional soil-growing and enable closer monitoring, so conditions can be optimised for maximum growth. Plants can also be stacked on top of each other to save space.

Aeroponics

Aeroponics involves growing plants in an air or mist environment. Plant roots are suspended in the air, and nutrient-rich water is routinely sprayed onto the roots.

Hydroponics

Hydroponics involves growing plants in mineral nutrient solutions. Plant roots are dangled into a basin containing a nutrient solution.

The New Green Revolution

During the **Green Revolution** of the mid-20th century, new agricultural technologies emerged. New seed strains were developed that increased crop yields. Chemical fertilisers and commercial farming further boosted productivity, but they also damaged the environment.

The current **New Green Revolution** aims to improve crop yields for LICs in a more sustainable way by educating people to:

- Breed highly pest- and drought-resistant plants
- Use genetic pest and disease control
- Employ crop rotation and nutrient cycling
- Use appropriate traditional farming methods

daydream
EDUCATION

Use of Biotechnology

Biotechnology involves improving production through genetic engineering.
Genetically modified (GM) crops have been manipulated for a variety of benefits, including:

Improved nutritional value of crops (e.g. rice with added vitamins)	Improved shelf life	Improved resistance to drought, pests and disease and reduced use of chemical pesticides	Improved flavour

The effects of GM foods on the environment and human health are still relatively unknown.
However, many people are worried about their effects on natural biodiversity and ecosystems.
As a result, their use is still very much limited, with several countries banning GM foods.

Appropriate Technology

Appropriate technology involves implementing practical farming methods that are suitable for the communities in which they will be used. Methods of appropriate technology in LICs include:

Drip irrigation using locally sourced materials

Renewable, locally available energy sources such as wind or solar power

Individual, human-powered water pumps

Large-Scale Agricultural Development: Almería, Spain

Almería in Spain is one of the driest parts of Europe, averaging only 200 mm of rain per year. Despite its arid environment, Almería's year-round warm climate enables crops, such as tomatoes and melons, to grow throughout the year.

The area around Almería has the world's largest concentration of greenhouses, which cover over 30,000 hectares. It produces over half of Europe's fruit and vegetables, generating over €1.2 billion per year.

✅ Advantages

- Seasonal fruit and vegetables can be grown all year round to serve local and global markets.
- Agriculture creates various employment opportunities, from low-skilled picking jobs to high-tech agribusiness jobs.
- New technologies, such as drip irrigation and hydroponics, have reduced the use of water and chemical pesticides.

❌ Disadvantages

- The plastic used to build the greenhouses has destroyed natural ecosystems, significantly damaging the local environment.
- Farming has put a strain on the local water supply, with local water stores drying up.
- Low-skilled workers, often illegal migrants, work in poor conditions and receive low wages.

 daydream EDUCATION

Photocopying or scanning this image is a breach of copyright law.

113

Sustainable Food Supply

The world's food supply needs to be managed sustainably to meet the demands of it's growing population and to ensure there is sufficient food for future generations.

Sustainable Food Production Methods

Organic Farming

Organic farming uses natural methods in place of chemical fertilisers, pesticides, herbicides and antibiotics to produce food. For example, natural fertilisers such as manure help to return nutrients and moisture to the soil, and natural forms of pest control maintain biodiversity.

Despite yielding less than inorganic farming methods, organic farming keeps soil fertile for use by future generations.

Permaculture

Permaculture is a system of agriculture and social design principles that is based on natural ecosystem processes.

It involves minimising the impact of agriculture on the natural environment, through buying and producing organic food, sourcing local produce, creating communities and eating seasonal food.

Urban Farming Initiatives

Urban farming initiatives bring farming to urbanised areas. Spaces to grow food and keep animals can be set up on allotments, green roofs, empty land and balconies.

Urban farming initiatives provide a sustainable way for families to eat fresh, healthy food that is produced cheaply and locally. It also provides an affordable option for low-income households.

Seasonal Food Consumption

People in HICs expect to be able to eat a wide variety of food all year round. For example, strawberries are harvested in the UK in summer, but to meet demand during the rest of the year, they are imported from countries such as Morocco and Egypt.

Eating seasonally reduces imports, 'food miles' and pollution.

daydream
EDUCATION

Meat and Fish from Sustainable Sources

Large-scale meat production is resource-intensive and damages the environment. It is also less sustainable than traditional farming.

Allowing livestock to graze on grassland reduces the amount of land required to grow grain crops to feed the livestock. Also, the natural manure produced by the livestock keeps the soil fertile.

Overfishing has a big impact on marine ecosystems and fish populations. For example, net fishing often catches unwanted species (bycatch), seriously depleting many fish populations, and dredging of the sea floor can destroy ecosystems.

Fishing quotas and fish farms help reduce the impact of fishing on ecosystems. Using dolphin-friendly nets or nets designed to catch only mature fish reduces the amount of bycatch.

Reduced Waste and Losses

Around one-third of food produced globally is lost or thrown away. In the UK, families throw away around £700 worth of food each year.

Food waste contributes to food insecurity, wastes energy used in production and increases greenhouse gas emissions from landfill.

Eating leftovers, using them for composting, planning meals better and freezing food are ways to reduce food waste and food insecurity.

Increasing Sustainable Food Supplies: Jamalpur, Bangladesh

- **Jamalpur** is located in northern Bangladesh.
- The area relies on agriculture for nearly 60% of its income.
- The region's main crops are rice, jute and wheat.

Historically, its population was food insecure because of unsustainable food production. However, intervention from the charity Practical Action helped improve food security by:

- **Implementing rice-fish culture** – Introducing fish to rice paddies provided the plants with natural fertiliser and helped circulate oxygen, improving plant growth. Rice yields increased and the fish provided people with a source of protein.
- **Using flood-resistant varieties of rice** – This made the food supply more reliable, improving the overall yields.
- **Planting fruit and vegetables on the dykes** – This increased dietary variety and the food supply.

To increase their incomes, local subsidence farmers could now sell any additional food produced. Practical Action reported that the average annual household income increased by nearly 400%, and that most families were now able to have three nutritionally balanced meals a day.

Fieldwork

Fieldwork involves applying geographical knowledge to real-world contexts. It enables learners to practise a range of skills outside the classroom and to gain new geographical insights into the world around them.

As part of the GCSE Geography course, you must undertake two geographical enquiries that examine contrasting **physical** and **human** environments. At least one must encompass the interaction between physical and human geography, and both must involve the collection of primary data.

There's no assessed coursework, but you will be asked about your fieldwork in your exam.

You will need to be able to answer questions about:

- Fieldwork techniques, such as data collection, and presentation methods and their usefulness.
- Your investigation, including your hypothesis, the data you collected, how you presented and analysed the data, and how you could improve your work.

 It is vital that you plan and prepare before carrying out your fieldwork. ☑

 Identifying your data collection methods beforehand will save a lot of time. ☑

Fieldwork Enquiry Process

1 Explaining the Focus of Your Enquiry

You need to be able to explain and justify:

Why you chose your question or hypothesis	The geographical idea or theory underpinning the enquiry	The risks associated with your enquiry and what you did to reduce them

2 Selecting, Measuring and Recording Data

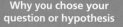

Primary Data	Secondary Data	Quantitative Data	Qualitative Data
Data that you or your group collected directly during your enquiry	Data from reviewed, published sources (e.g. journal articles)	Data that has a numerical value (e.g. age, distance)	Data that does not have a numerical value (e.g. colour, texture)

You need to be able to explain and justify:

- What data you collected and how it addressed your question or hypothesis. Both primary and secondary data should be included, as should quantitative and qualitative data.

- How you recorded and measured your data. For example: *We used personal data collection sheets and questionnaires to record our findings.*

- How these data collection methods were appropriate for your chosen enquiry. For example: *We used photographs for data collection because they provided visual evidence of coastal erosion, including erosional landforms such as stacks and arches.*

- The sampling methods used and why they were appropriate for your chosen enquiry. For example: *I used transects to sample sediment. This method allowed me to examine evidence for different types of sediment, and their shape and size, within a representative area of the coast.*

daydream
EDUCATION

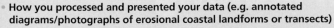

3 Processing and Presenting the Data

You need to be able to explain:

- How you processed and presented your data (e.g. annotated diagrams/photographs of erosional coastal landforms or transects)
- Why the presentational methods used were appropriate for your chosen enquiry
- How you ensured your data was accurate and appropriate
- How data can be presented in different ways to make inferences and comparisons easier
- How else you could have presented your own data

4 Analysing, Describing and Explaining Your Data

You need to be able to explain:

| Your data, and a general overview of what it showed | How you analysed your data | Any links or anomolies that you were able to identify in your data |

5 Drawing Conclusions and Summaries

You need to be able to explain:

- How the data in your enquiry answered your question, or supported or rejected your hypothesis

6 Evaluating the Enquiry

You need to be able to explain:

| Any problems with your data collection methods | Any limitations with the data collected | Any additional data which may have been useful | How reliable your conclusions are |

What Types Of Questions Can You Expect In The Exam?

You will be faced with a range of questions relating to general fieldwork techniques and your own investigations. Some examples are shown below.

- Suggest one way in which the data technique shown in Figure X can be made more reliable.
- State the title of your enquiry in which physical geography data was collected.
- Assess how effective your presentation technique(s) were in representing the data collected in this enquiry.
- For one of your geographical enquiries, to what extent were results of this enquiry helpful in reaching a reliable conclusion?

 Remember to demonstrate your geographical knowledge throughout your exam, using geographical terminology and relating your results to core geographical theory.

Decision Making

What Will This Part of the Exam Involve?

It will involve interpreting information from resources and applying geographical knowledge from the course to analyse an issue, explore solutions, and make and justify a decision. Topics included in the exam will be from your course and will involve both **human** and **physical** geography.

For the exam, a resource booklet will be issued to you. If you received this before your exam, you will not be allowed to take an annotated copy in with you. Instead, you will be issued with a fresh copy. Therefore, it is important that you study and familiarise yourself with the information carefully. Additional research and understanding about the issues will be rewarded in the exam where it adds value to an answer.

What Will the Resource Booklet Include?

The resource booklet will contain a mix of geographical resources. These may include:

- Maps
- Photographs
- Satellite images
- Diagrams
- Statistics
- Graphs
- Newspaper articles
- Quotes from different stakeholders

What Kinds of Questions Should I Expect?

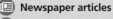

1. Skills Questions

These will require you to apply your geographical skills to answer short questions relating to the resources. For example:

0 2 . 3 In how many countries shown in **Figure 3** is it estimated that 81–90% of the urban population live in slums? **[1 mark]**

2. Extended Writing Questions

These questions will also be based on the resources. They will require you to analyse the resources and use your own geographical knowledge to explain your answer. For example:

0 3 . 2 Study **Figure 5**, 'Urban problems in Kolkata – improving the lives of the urban poor', in the resource booklet.

Suggest why people living in cities in LICs/NEEs, such as Kolkata, are more vulnerable to natural hazards than people living in cities in HICs. Use **Figure 5** and your own understanding to support your answer. **[6 marks]**

3. Decision-Making Exercises

These will require you to argue your point of view on an issue, using the information in your resources to support your decision. You will need to apply your own geographical understanding and show that you have considered all possible options, stakeholder views, and advantages and disadvantages to come to a well-balanced conclusion.

0 3 . 2 Three projects have been suggested to try and improve the quality of life for the urban poor in Kolkata. These are described in **Figure 5**.

Which of the three projects do you think will improve the socio-economic and environmental conditions for the urban poor of Kolkata most effectively?

Use evidence from the resource booklet and your own understanding to explain why you have reached this decision. **[9 marks]**

Remember: In the decision-making exercise, you should consider how your decision will affect humans (both socially and economically) and the environment. You should also suggest ways to reduce negative impacts.

daydream EDUCATION

Geographical Skills

Latitude and Longitude

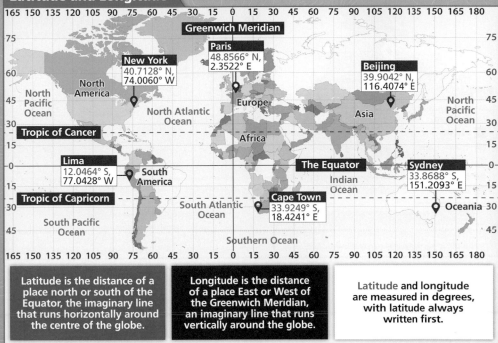

Greenwich Meridian

Paris
48.8566° N,
2.3522° E

New York
40.7128° N,
74.0060° W

Beijing
39.9042° N,
116.4074° E

North America

North Pacific Ocean

Europe

Asia

North Pacific Ocean

North Atlantic Ocean

Tropic of Cancer

Africa

Lima
12.0464° S,
77.0428° W

South America

The Equator

Sydney
33.8688° S,
151.2093° E

Indian Ocean

Tropic of Capricorn

Cape Town
33.9249° S,
18.4241° E

South Atlantic Ocean

Oceania

South Pacific Ocean

Southern Ocean

Latitude is the distance of a place north or south of the Equator, the imaginary line that runs horizontally around the centre of the globe.

Longitude is the distance of a place East or West of the Greenwich Meridian, an imaginary line that runs vertically around the globe.

Latitude and longitude are measured in degrees, with latitude always written first.

Dot Maps

2010 US Population Dot Density Map
(each dot represents 500,000 people)

A dot map uses dots to visually represent the spatial distribution of a feature or phenomenon. A dot represents a certain number of features or phenomena. The more dots there are, the greater the number of features or phenomena.

Proportional Symbols

European Foresty Production by Country, 2006

Key

Forestry Production in million cubic meters

65.6

32.4

15.7

0.3

Proportional symbols are symbols or shapes of different sizes that represent different quantities. The larger the symbol, the greater the quantity.

daydream EDUCATION

Choropleth Maps

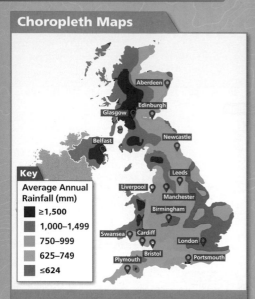

Key

Average Annual Rainfall (mm)

- ≥1,500
- 1,000–1,499
- 750–999
- 625–749
- ≤624

Choropleth maps visually display patterns or variation across a geographic area. They use different shades, colours or patterns to represent ranges of values.

Isolines

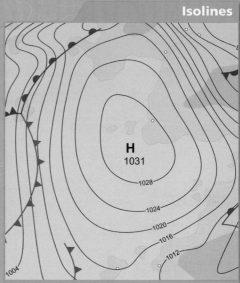

Isolines link areas that share a common value. Lines are often labelled with their value. Contour lines join points of equal altitude whereas isobars, on a weather map, join places of equal atmospheric pressure.

Flow Lines

Key

Average Flow in cubic feet per second (cfs)

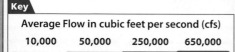

10,000   50,000   250,000   650,000

Flow lines show the volume of movement between places with the lines being proportional in width to the volume of the flow. Where required, direction is indicated by arrows. These may sometimes be slightly stylised.

Desire Lines

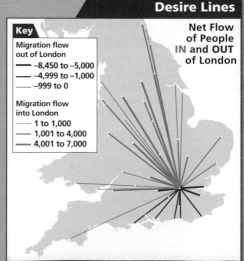

Net Flow of People IN and OUT of London

Key

Migration flow out of London
- −8,450 to −5,000
- −4,999 to −1,000
- −999 to 0

Migration flow into London
- 1 to 1,000
- 1,001 to 4,000
- 4,001 to 7,000

Desire lines are similar to flow lines. They use straight lines to show movement from one place to another. The thickness of the lines varies to represent the volume, or desirability, of movement.

daydream
EDUCATION

Ordnance Survey (OS) is a national mapping agency in the United Kingdom.

Common Map Symbols

Roads	Railway	Boundaries	Natural Features	Other
M1 **Motorway**	**Multiple track**	→ — → — **National**	☐ **Water**	☐ **Building**
A35 **Dual carriageway**	**Single track**	**County**	☐ **Mud**	♱ ♰ **Places of worship**
A30 **Main road**	**Station**	**National park**	☐ **Sand**	P **Parking**
B30 **Secondary road**			🌲 **Woodland**	V **Visitor centres**

Direction

Direction is shown by the points on a compass, with the four cardinal directions being **north (N)**, **east (E)**, **south (S)** and **west (W)**. A compass always points to magnetic north.

An easy way to remember the order clockwise from north is 'Naughty Elephants Squirt Water'.

Scale and Distance

Maps show an area reduced in size. This is measured using a scale, which is the ratio of a model dimension to the real-life dimension. Ordnance Survey map scales include:

Explorer Maps 1:25,000 1 cm = 0.25 km (250 m)	Landranger Maps 1:50,000 1 cm = 0.5 km (500 m)	Travel Maps 1:125,000 1 cm = 1.25 km (1,250 m)

The map below has a scale of 1:50,000. This means that the map is 50,000 times smaller than the actual area.

On the map, the campsite is 2 cm from the church. To calculate the actual distance, multiply the measurement by the scale:

2 cm × Scale
2 cm × 50,000 = **100,000 cm**

Convert the measurement to the correct unit:

100,000 cm = **1 km**

Therefore, the campsite is 1 km from the church.

Grid References

Maps often include a grid, which makes it is easier to find a specific point or area.

The numbers on the vertical lines are called eastings. The numbers up the horizontal lines are called northings. Eastings are always written before the northings when stating grid references.

Four-Figure Grid References

To find the four-figure grid reference for Diggory's Island...

- Find the easting value for the line directly to the left of the island. This is 84.

- Find the northing value for the line directly below the island. This is 70.

- Therefore, the four-figure grid reference for Diggory's Island is 8470.

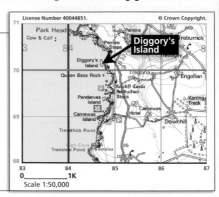

Six-Figure Grid References

To find the six-figure grid reference for Diggory's Island...

- Split this four-figure grid reference square into a 10 x 10 grid, and work out the easting and northing values within this grid. The easting is 7, and the northing is 1.

- Add these easting and northing values to the end of the original easting (84) and northing (70) values. The new easting is 847, and the new northing is 701.

- Therefore, the six-figure grid reference for Diggory's Island is 847701.

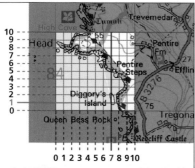

Relief

The relief of land is shown on maps using contour lines and spot heights.

Contour lines join points of equal altitude, or height above or below sea level. They are usually spaced at 5- or 10-metre intervals, so the steepness of terrain can be determined. The closer the contour lines, the steeper the land.

A spot height shows the altitude of an exact point on a map. It is represented by a black dot with its elevation listed beside it.

Triangulation pillars are surveying stations that were erected by the OS to help it create mapping systems. These were often set up at the highest point in an area.

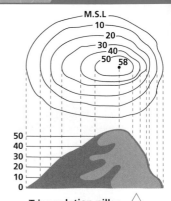

Triangulation pillar

daydream EDUCATION

Bar Charts

A bar chart is used to display qualitative and categorical numerical data. Data is represented by different sized bars. When drawing bar charts:

- Give the graph a title.
- Label both axes.
- Use equal intervals on the axes.
- Leave a gap between each bar.

What was Japan's GDP in 2016?

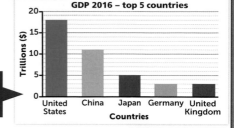

Composite

A composite bar chart displays proportions, with each bar split into categories.

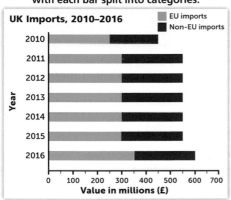

What was the value of imports from the EU in 2015?

Dual

A dual bar chart displays two sets of data for comparison.

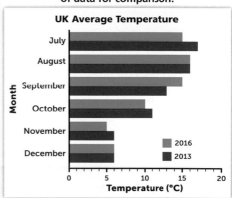

What was the difference between the average UK temperature in July 2013 and July 2016?

Pictograms

A pictogram uses pictures to represent data. All pictures must be the same.

Wheat Production by Country (2014)

Country		Frequency
Canada	🌾	29
China	🌾🌾🌾🌾🌾🌾	126
France	🌾🌾	39
Germany	🌾	27
India	🌾🌾🌾🌾🌾	94
Pakistan	🌾	26
Russia	🌾🌾🌾	60
USA	🌾🌾🌾	55

🌾 = 20 million tonnes

How much more wheat did Russia produce than Germany?

Histograms

A histogram displays continuous data. Unlike other bar charts, there are no gaps between the bars.

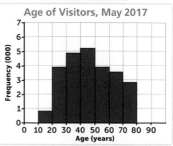

How many visitors were between 40 and 50 years old?

daydream EDUCATION

Line Graphs

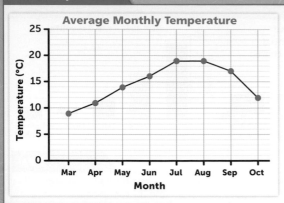

Line graphs are used to display continuous data and help show trends or change over time.

In a line graph, data is plotted as a series of points that are joined with straight lines.

Always ensure that your line graph has a title and that the axes are labelled and use equal intervals.

What was the average monthly temperature in June?

Pie Charts

A pie chart is a circular chart that is split into sections to show proportion. The table below shows data on primary fuels. Follow the steps to create a pie chart for this data.

Step 1. In a pie chart, data is represented as a proportion of 360, as there are 360° in a circle. Therefore, to calculate the proportion for each primary fuel type, divide 360 by the total amount of primary fuel: 360 ÷ 125 = 2.88.

Indigenous Production of Primary Fuels in the UK, 2016

Fuel	Frequency (million tonnes of oil equivalent)	Frequency × 2.88	Proportion of 360
Coal	2.5	2.5 × 2.88 = 7.2	7.2
Petrol	52.0	52.0 × 2.88 = 149.8	149.8
Nautral gas	39.8	39.8 × 2.88 = 114.6	114.6
Bioenergy & waste	10.7	10.7 × 2.88 = 30.8	30.8
Nuclear	15.4	15.4 × 2.88 = 44.4	44.4
Wind, solar & hydro	4.6	4.6 × 2.88 = 13.2	13.2
Total	125	125 × 2.88 = 360	360

Step 2. To calculate the proportion for each fuel, multiply its frequency by 2.88.

2.5 × 2.88 = 7.2

Step 3. Now that the fuels have been converted to proportions of 360, the pie chart can be drawn.

Start by drawing a straight line from the centre of the circle to the edge.

Use a protractor to measure and mark the angle for each fuel, and label them accordingly.

Wind, solar & hydro
Coal
13.2°
7.2°
Nuclear
Bioenergy & waste 44.4°
30.8°
149.8°
Petrol
114.6°
Natural gas

daydream
EDUCATION

Population Pyramids

A population pyramid shows the various age groups in a population, based on gender.

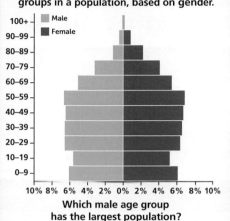

Which male age group has the largest population?

Dispersion Diagrams

A dispersion diagram shows each data value plotted as an individual point against a scale or set of variables.

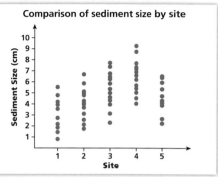

Which site is most likely to be located nearest to the source of the river?

Scatter Graphs

Scatter graphs are used to show how closely two sets of data are related.
Correlation describes how the two sets of data are related.

Positive Correlation	Negative Correlation	No Correlation
When the plotted points go upward from left to right, there is a positive correlation.	When the plotted points go downward from left to right, there is negative correlation.	When there is no relationship between two data sets, there is no correlation.

GDP per Head vs Life Expectancy

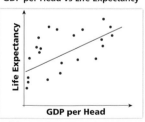

Altitude vs Temperature

Household Income vs Divorce Rates

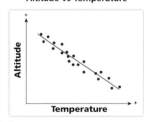

This graph shows that there is a positive correlation between GDP per head and life expectancy. As GDP per head increases, so does life expectancy.	This graph shows that there is a negative correlation between altitude and temperature. As altitude increases, temperature decreases.	This graph shows that there is no correlation between household income and divorce rates.

Line of Best Fit
A line of best fit is a line that is drawn through the centre group of data points.
When the plotted points are close to the line, there is strong correlation.
When they are spread out on either side of the line, there is moderate correlation.

Central Tendency

Central tendency is a single value that is representative of a whole data set.
The mean, mode and median are the most common measures of central tendency.

The table below shows the daily rainfall totals (mm) for 11 days in January.

| 4.2 | 9.6 | 4.2 | 0 | 8.2 | 4.6 | 5.7 | 0.3 | 0.2 | 11.1 | 8.4 |

Mean

The mean is the sum of values divided by the number of values.

$$\text{Mean} = \frac{\text{sum of values}}{\text{number of values}}$$

The mean daily rainfall was:

$$\text{Mean} = \frac{4.2 + 9.6 + 4.2 + 0 + 8.2 + 4.6 + 5.7 + 0.3 + 0.2 + 11.1 + 8.4}{11} = 5.14$$

Mode

The mode is the value that occurs most often.
The mode daily rainfall was 4.2 because it was the only value to occur twice.

Median

The median is the middle value when the data is arranged in order of size.

| 0 | 0.2 | 0.3 | 4.2 | 4.2 | 4.6 | 5.7 | 8.2 | 8.4 | 9.6 | 11.1 |

The position of the median value can be calculated using the following formula:

$$\text{Median} = \frac{\text{number of values} + 1}{2} = \frac{11 + 1}{2} = \frac{12}{2} = 6$$

The median is the 6th item in the list, which is 4.6.

If there is an even number of values, the median is the mean of the two middle values.

Range

The **range** is the difference between the lowest and highest values in a data set.

0 ← range = 11.1 → 11.1

The **interquartile range** is the difference between the lower quartile and the upper quartile.

| 0 | 0.2 | 0.3 | 4.2 | 4.2 | 4.6 | 5.7 | 8.2 | 8.4 | 9.6 | 11.1 |

The lower quartile is the median of the bottom half of the data.

The upper quartile is the median of the upper half of the data.

0.3 ← interquartile range = 8.4 − 0.3 = 8.1 → 8.4

daydream
EDUCATION

Calculating Percentages

Percentages are used to express how large or small one quantity is relative to another quantity.

The population of Japan in 2016 was 127 million, including an urban population of 99 million. What was Japan's urban population as a percentage of its total population in 2016?

1. Divide the urban population by the total population.

$$\frac{99}{127} = 0.78$$

2. Multiply the answer by 100.

$$0.78 \times 100 = 78$$

In 2016, 78% of Japan's population lived in urban areas.

Calculating Percentage Change

$$\text{Percentage change} = \frac{\text{Change in value}}{\text{Original value}} \times 100$$

In 2015, Ethiopia's GDP was approximately $64 billion. In 2016, it increased to $72 billion.

Calculate the percentage change in Ethiopia's GDP.

1 Calculate the change in value.

$$72 - 64 = 8$$

2 Divide the change in value by the original value.

$$8 \div 72 = 0.11$$

3 Multiply by 100.

$$0.11 \times 100 = 11$$

Ethiopia's GDP increased by 11%.

Percentage Increase

In 2017 the world population was 7.6 billion. It is estimated this will increase by 22% by 2050. If estimates are correct, what will the world population be in 2050?

1 Calculate 22% of 7.6 billion.

$$0.22 \times 7.6 = 1.672$$

2 Add your answer to the original amount.

$$7.6 + 1.672 = 9.272$$

If the world population grows by 22%, the population will be 9.272 billion.

Percentage Decrease

The UK government has committed to reducing greenhouse gas emissions by at least 80% of 1990 levels by 2050. If it achieves this goal, what will its emissions be if 1990 emissions were 800 $MtCO_2e$?

1 Calculate 80% of 800.

$$0.8 \times 800 = 640$$

2 Subtract your answer from the original amount.

$$800 - 640 = 160$$

If greenhouse gas emissions are reduced by 80%, they will be 160 $MtCO_2e$.

daydream EDUCATION

Notes

Index

Index